T0360497

Global Business Cycles and Developing Countries

This book investigates how global business cycles impact the economies of developing countries. Global business cycles, the wave-like movements of economic expansion followed by contraction in aggregate economic activities, impact all economies comprising the global economy. The patterns being shown in developing countries correspond increasingly to those in the global north, yet there is a relative dearth of studies exploring whether global business cycles exist and how they operate in developing economies.

This book explores how cycles operate at the global level and in developing countries, with a particular focus on the level of development and the structure of the economy. Drawing an important distinction between cycles and fluctuations, the book criticises mainstream conceptualisation and identification of cycle phenomena, and instead proposes an alternative conception and methodology for the identification of cycles. Along the way, the book also delves into the manufacturing and rise of China in the industrial arena, as increasingly important drivers of global business cycles and global economic growth.

This book will be an important read for researchers and upper-level students of development economics and international political economy.

Eri Ikeda is an Assistant Professor in the Department of Management Studies, Indian Institute of Technology, Delhi, India.

Routledge Explorations in Development Studies

This Development Studies series features innovative and original research at the regional and global scale. It promotes interdisciplinary scholarly works drawing on a wide spectrum of subject areas, in particular politics, health, economics, rural and urban studies, sociology, environment, anthropology, and conflict studies.

Topics of particular interest are globalization; emerging powers; children and youth; cities; education; media and communication; technology development; and climate change.

In terms of theory and method, rather than basing itself on any orthodoxy, the series draws broadly on the tool kit of the social sciences in general, emphasizing comparison, the analysis of the structure and processes, and the application of qualitative and quantitative methods.

Engendering Transformative Thinking and Practice in International Development
Gillian Fletcher

New Donors on the Postcolonial Crossroads
Eastern Europe and Western Aid
Tomáš Profant

The Power of Civil Society in the Middle East and North Africa
Peace-building, Change, and Development
Edited by Ibrahim Natil, Chiara Pierobon, and Lilian Tauber

Global Business Cycles and Developing Countries
Eri Ikeda

For more information about this series, please visit: https://www.routledge.com

Global Business Cycles and Developing Countries

Eri Ikeda

LONDON AND NEW YORK

First published 2020
by Routledge
2 Park Square, Milton Park, Abingdon, Oxon OX14 4RN

and by Routledge
52 Vanderbilt Avenue, New York, NY 10017

Routledge is an imprint of the Taylor & Francis Group, an informa business

British Library Cataloguing-in-Publication Data
A catalogue record for this book is available from the British Library

Library of Congress Cataloging-in-Publication Data
Names: Ikeda, Eri, author.
Title: Global business cycles and developing countries / Eri Ikeda.
Description: First Edition. | New York: Routledge, 2019. |
Series: Routledge explorations in development studies |
Includes bibliographical references and index. |
Identifiers: LCCN 2019029834 (print) | LCCN 2019029835 (ebook) |
ISBN 9780367338640 (hardback) | ISBN 9780429322495 (ebook)
Subjects: LCSH: Business cycles—Developing countries. |
Economic development—Developing countries.
Classification: LCC HB3711 .I484 2019 (print) | LCC HB3711 (ebook) |
DDC 338.5/42091724—dc23
LC record available at https://lccn.loc.gov/2019029834
LC ebook record available at https://lccn.loc.gov/2019029835

ISBN: 978-0-367-33864-0 (hbk)
ISBN: 978-0-429-32249-5 (ebk)

Typeset in Times New Roman
by codeMantra

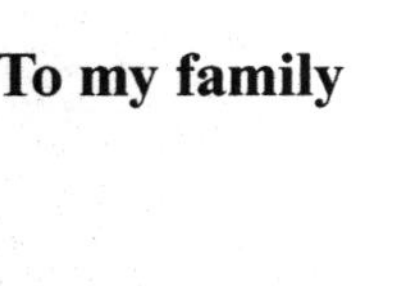

To my family

Contents

Figures

Tables

Preface and acknowledgements

This book is the outcome of research on *business cycles* for almost ten years, including doctoral research. This long gestation period allowed me to embark on the journey to understand the functioning of the global economic system that I have long been interested in. Yet, understanding the business cycle phenomena has been a daunting task. In the end, the task only became manageable by narrowing the focus and research objectives; specifically this book mainly sought to ascertain the existence of a global business cycle and its country drivers, with a view to establishing and understanding the existence and movements of cyclical phenomena in developing countries.

While the business cycle has not been a fashionable subject for an academic research for at least the last two decades, and certainly not in the realm of development studies, the importance of the subject is clearly evident and will grow not only under the current and future global economic conditions, associated with the rapid structural shift in the global economy, but also to prepare for the next global recession. Needless to say, more work needs to be done both to fill the gaps of the present study and to expand the scope of the business cycle analyses, but I still hope this book manages to convey something worthwhile to make a contribution to the existing knowledge of business cycles.

This book could not have materialised without the invaluable and arduous supervision and mentorship by Dr. Howard Nicholas. He gave me the confidence to believe that getting to grips with this discipline was not beyond me. My heartfelt and deepest thanks go to him before anyone else.

A number of academic staff members, internal and external supervisors, doctoral committee members, administrative staff members, colleagues, and friends also supported and encouraged me by providing insights, feedback, expertise, technical assistance, spaces, and opportunities, and helped me to overcome many hurdles. I thank all of them, and especially would like to express my sincere appreciation to Dr. Servaas Storm, Prof. Arjun Bedi, all my good friends, Paula Bownas (thesis editor), and Nicolien. I would like to also thank the Japan-IMF scholarship Program for Advanced Studies (JISP) for financial support for two years and internship opportunity.

Last but not least, I would like to express my special and sincere appreciation to my family in Japan for accepting and supporting me in pursuing the path that I chose.

Abbreviations

ABC	Austrian Business Cycle
ADF	Augmented Dickey-Fuller (test)
BB(Q)	Bry and Boschan (Quarterly) method
BP	Band-Pass (filter)
DSGE	Dynamic Stochastic General Equilibrium (model)
EBC	Equilibrium Business Cycle
ECRI	Economic Cycle Research Institute
EDA	Exploratory Data Analysis
EU	European Union
FED	Federal Reserve System
FRED	Federal Reserve Economic Data
G7	Group of Seven
GDP	Gross Domestic Product
GNI	Gross National Income
GNP	Gross National Product
HP	Hodrick-Prescott (filter)
IMF	International Monetary Fund
MENA	Middle East and North Africa region
MS	Markov-switching (model)
NBER	(U.S.) National Bureau of Economic Research
OECD	Organisation for Economic Co-operation and Development
OLS	Ordinary Least Squares
PAT	Phase Average Trend
RBC	Real Business Cycle
UBS	Union Bank of Switzerland
U.K.	United Kingdom
U.S.	United States of America
VAR	Vector Auto Regression
WB	World Bank
WDI	World Development Indicators

1 Introduction

The phenomena of business cycles[1] can be defined as alternating periods of expansionary and contractionary economic activity (see Figure 1.1). The particular focus of this book is such cycles at global and sub-global (those deemed to pertain to various groupings or clusters of countries comprising the global economy) levels, with a particular attention to developing countries. The main reason of this focus is to seek to contribute to filling the lacuna in our understanding of cycles at the global level and in developing countries and, in the process, to aid the development of the general corpus of knowledge in the field of business cycle research.

The study of these phenomena has a long history,[2] with periods of renewed interest typically following major economic and/or financial crises. A case in point is the severe economic and financial crisis experienced by most economies between 2007 and 2009. This has rekindled interest in business cycle research in both policy and academic circles in many countries. Indeed, up until this crisis, and certainly for much of the 1990s and the first part of the 2000s (the period often referred to

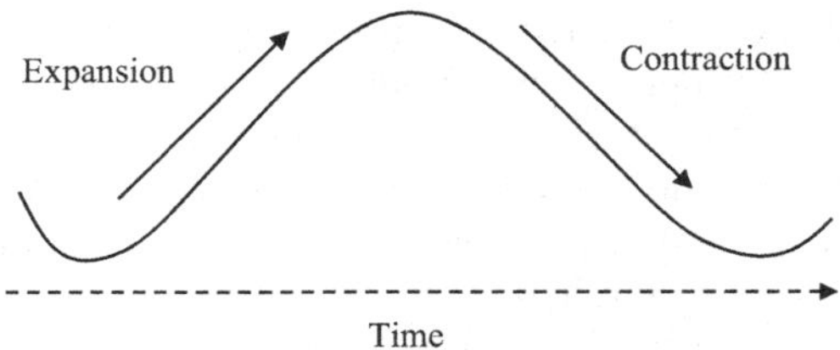

Figure 1.1 Generic cycle.

Note: Generic cycles refer to the abstract or general characterisation of cycles. The label for the Y axis of this figure depends on the variable used to depict business cycle activity. The most common is the real GDP growth rate.

as the 'Great Moderation'), there was something of a decline in interest in these phenomena, with many claiming the taming and death of the cycle, as a result of various structural changes in the economy and successful government interventionist (or even liberalisation) policies.[3] Many prominent economists declared the success of mainstream macroeconomic thinking in tackling the repeated episodes of depression and recession (see Krugman, 2009). To quote one prominent economist, Olivier J. Blanchard, on the eve of the 2008 financial crisis: 'the state of macro is good' (2008, p. 2), while the renowned U.S. economist Robert E. Lucas. Jr. (2003, p. 1) boasted that the 'central problem of depression prevention has been solved, for all practical purposes, and has in fact been solved for many decades'.

It is not only academics that are starting to become aware of the importance of studying business cycles at both national and global levels but also, and perhaps more importantly, policy makers. Specifically, there appears to be a growing awareness of the synchronised economic movements in the global economy (see, for example, International Monetary Fund [IMF], 2019[4]), and the success or failure of their economic policies depends to a large extent on their understanding of business cycle phenomena.[5]

Most research on business cycles has focused on the advanced countries, especially the United States, Europe, and Japan.[6] Little, if any, attention has been paid to the analysis of similar cycles in developing countries, regardless of their strong economic growth as well as growing presence in the global economy in the last three decades. Indeed, the study of business cycles in developing countries remains rudimentary. There are, however, signs that this is now changing, at least in part because of the growing importance of many of these economies, most notably China, in the global economy. The Chair of the U.S. Federal Reserve at the time, Janet L. Yellen, stated in her speech on the outlook for the U.S. economy that '[o]ne concern pertains to the pace of global growth, which is importantly influenced by developments in China' (Yellen, 2016; see also 2015a). More recently, Managing Director of the IMF, Christine Lagarde said in January 2019 at the World Economic Forum, '[s]hould the slowdown [of China] be excessively fast, it would constitute a real issue both domestically and probably on a more systemic basis' (Reid, 2019).[7]

Against this background, the aim of book is twofold. One is to ascertain the existence of business cycles in developing countries (to identify them and understand their nature), and the other is to establish the fundamental drivers being external global forces, i.e., global business cycles. With the understanding that these aspects are conditioned by the conception and definition of cycles, this book also pays particular attention to this pivotal element.

In this regard, this book intends to mainly argue the following five key points. First, as opposed to the mainstream view of cycles as 'fluctuations', cycles are recurrent, non-periodic, and non-symmetric alternating periods of expansion and contraction in economic activity. This is the foundations for understanding all observable cycle phenomena, i.e., cycles at the global level and pertaining to groupings of developing countries.[8] Although observed cyclical phenomena may vary over time and location, it is argued that they all share certain common characteristics; those depicted by the generic cycles (see more details in Figure 1.1 and Chapter 3).[9]

Second, given the first point above, the identification of business cycles cannot be based on the mechanical application of rigid mathematical formula and econometric models. Thus, there is a need for the alternative identification method.

Third, cyclical patterns are evident in a growing number of developing countries, as is their increasing synchronisation with the leading global economies and one another. Hence, the phenomena of global and sub-global business cycles can be said to exist.

Fourth, the nature of business cycles (especially timing of the occurrence, duration, and amplitude) in developing countries varies depending on their trend growth rates, economic structures, and levels of development.

Lastly, the main drivers of global business cycles are cycles in global manufacturing activities, not the advanced ('high-income') economies, and the main drivers of cycles in the developing ('middle- and low-income') countries are cycles in the global economy.

The approach adopted in this book will comprise, for the first part, a critical review of the literature on conceptions of cycles, methods of their identification, and their drivers, with a view to developing a basis for the following analyses; for the second part, a presentation of an alternative conception of cycles and corresponding method for their identification; and, lastly, an alternative view of their drivers. The literature reviewed is for the most part that deemed to be the orthodox or mainstream literature on business cycles.[10] Much of this can be argued to fall under the umbrella of the so-called Neoclassical school of thought.[11] The critical aspect of the review will be in terms of theoretical logic and supporting empirical evidence of the mainstream cycle analyses from the non-mainstream view. For empirical analyses, there is a clear preference among those analysing business cycles for a deductive rather than inductive approach, making use of a variety of quantitative methods. Among them, the main methodology adopted in this book is exploratory data analysis (EDA),[12] and other statistical methods such as correlation and econometric analyses in support of EDA findings where applicable, placing emphasis on a prior theoretical reasoning.[13] In keeping with this emphasis, econometric analyses take close account of the *economic* significance of the results, and not simply *statistical* significance.[14] This approach is different from the widely applied mainstream approach that exclusively relies on mathematical modelling and econometric method (often a-theoretic in nature[15]),[16] given very different conception of cycles; non-regular and recurrent movements in economic activity. Most of these existing (empirically testable) mainstream methodologies typically assume, and indeed must assume, that cycles, if they exist, recur with a fixed periodicity and symmetry (see more details, Chapter 2).

The data used for the study are entirely macroeconomic in nature. They are drawn mostly from the World Bank's World Development Indicators (WDI) database to ensure as much consistency and availability as possible given the large array of countries included in the study. These data are supplemented by those drawn from other international organisations such as the IMF, and the Organisation for Economic Co-operation and Development (OECD), as well as various national sources such as central banks (e.g., U.S. Federal Reserve System) and statistics bureaus as and when necessary. The frequency of data is for the most part annual, except those in sections on identification and existence of business cycles in Chapter 2, and county drivers of global cycles in Chapter 5. It is important to note that the availability of relevant macroeconomic data varies between countries and their levels of development. Thus, as is to be expected, longer and higher frequency (i.e., quarterly, monthly, and daily) series of relevant data are more readily available for advanced than for developing countries;[17] there are also considerable differences between individual developing countries. For advanced countries relevant data for the present study are available from as far back as the early 1960s, while for a majority of developing countries they are only available from the 1970s or even the 1980s onwards, depending on the variables concerned. It is also certainly recognised that use of higher frequency data allows the researcher to capture macroeconomic developments taking place much earlier than is possible with the use of lower frequency data, but it is considered that the lack of availability of longer periods for these data, especially for developing countries, outweighs these benefits. The use of quarterly data used in the literature review is, incidentally, to permit an assessment of the findings of studies of cycles in the U.S. economy using this frequency of data.[18]

As has been the case with most empirical studies of business cycles, considerable use will be made of Gross Domestic Product (GDP) data, particularly GDP at current market prices, current U.S. dollars, and constant local currency units.[19] Also, as with other studies, considerable attention will be paid to economic growth rates, since these are seen as pivotal for identifying and analysing cycles. GDP data series are used in the present study in spite of the many known problems arising from the construction of these data, ranging from the omission of large parts of the economic activity of countries to outright fraud in surveys and estimates used in their construction (see more details in Chapter 2).

Data for the global economy and country groupings based on the levels of development and the structure of the economy are constructed using appropriate aggregation methods (see also Chapters 4 and 5 for the details). Since considerable attention is paid to the global economy as a composite in this study, the question arises as to how this composite is to be derived. Although data on the global economy as a composite are available from certain of the above-mentioned international data sources (typically under the label of 'world' composite), the manner of their construction does not entirely suit the purposes of the present study—hence the construction in this study of alternative global economy composites. One problem faced in this construction has been the availability of data. As noted above, data availability varies between countries according to their levels of development. The solution adopted in the present study is to include as many countries as possible assuming that the omitted countries will have little or no bearing on the resulting composites and analytical results derived from their use.

As should already be apparent, an important distinction in the present study is between so-called advanced (/developed) and developing (/emerging) countries (/economies). As a number of researchers have commented, it is not entirely clear where one should draw the line between advanced and developing countries (see Nielsen, 2011; Khokhar and Serajuddin, 2015). Since the precise demarcation line between these countries is of little consequence for the analysis undertaken here, this study will adopt the conventional and widely used classifications of these groupings, using income levels provided by the World Bank. Specifically, the countries classified as high-income by the World Bank are considered to be the advanced countries, and the non-high-income countries (i.e., middle- and low-income countries) as the developing countries.[20]

Distinctions are also drawn in the present study between groupings of developing countries based on economic structures. The economic structures considered important in the present study are those pertaining to the sub-components of GDP. These are typically seen as agriculture, industry, and services, with important distinctions between sub-components of these aggregates, including that between the manufacturing and non-manufacturing sub-components of industry. Since these distinctions are not systematically used to organise the country data provided by the World Bank and other organisations noted above, they are constructed as and when required in the present study. Particular attention is paid to the sub-components which form the basis for important exports of developing countries, viz., manufactures and non-manufactures comprised of primary commodities (food, fuel, ores and metals, and agricultural raw materials).

A number of caveats must be noted with respect to the present study. First of all, its focus is exclusively on the phenomenon of the business cycle and not macroeconomic phenomena in general. While it is recognised that the two are linked, it is felt that locating the analysis of cycles in the broader corpus of macroeconomy will result in an unnecessary digression.

Second, although there are no doubt considerable differences between the various sub-schools comprising the mainstream and non-mainstream approach, including in respect of their understandings of business cycles, each sub-group is treated as one homogeneous grouping for the purposes of this study. Since the aim is to derive certain fundamental shared elements of these approach to the understanding of cycles at the global and sub-global levels for reasons given above, it is felt that such divisions that exist between the sub-schools with respect to the analyses of cycles are of no consequence for the purposes of the present study.

Third, reference has already been made above to the data limitations faced by studies such as the present one, which are concerned with the macroeconomic dynamics of developing countries, but this warrants repeating here. Specifically, it is important to note that such limitations in terms of the quality of data provided by many developing countries make it necessary to be cautious about drawing hard and fast conclusions from analyses of these data.

Fourth, this book will not cover the analyses on sub-divided clusters within the sub-global groupings of developing countries (i.e., clusters pertaining to middle- and low-income countries for the level of development, and food, fuel, ores and metals, and agricultural raw materials exporting countries for the structure of the economy) and individual developing countries (for the identification of these cycles, see Ikeda, 2018). Since this study is of the view that the global economy as integrated economies (see Chapters 2 and 3 for more details), above-mentioned sub-divided clusters and individual country cycles could be, and should be, conceived to one degree or another with reference to the global cycles and cycles pertaining to sub-global groupings of countries.

Fifth, although the literature on business cycles identifies cycles of many different time durations, ranging from the long wave of 60 years to the inventory cycle of 2–3 years, the present study will focus on what has been referred to as the Juglar cycle—the duration of which is seen to be some 7–11 years (see Schumpeter, 1939).[21] This is because the existence of the Juglar cycle is accepted by most cycle economists and tends to be the focus of most research on the subject. This is not to deny the existence of other cycles, most notably the so-called long wave or K-wave, named after the Russian economist, Nicolai Kondratieff, who is credited with its discovery by those subscribing to its existence.[22]

Sixth, the explanation of the drivers of cycles in the present study has a somewhat different focus from the majority of explanations of such drivers. Specifically, no attempt is made to determine the drivers of cycles in general, i.e., the cause of generic cycles and their transmission mechanism between selected countries, which is the traditional focus of most studies of drivers of cycles in the business cycle literature (see, for example, Ikeda, 2012 for a review of these studies).[23] Rather, the focus of this book is the country drivers of global cycles (viz., which countries are the most important drivers of the global cycle and why?), and the external drivers of cycles in developing countries. The reason for this focus is its perceived theoretical and policy importance (see Chapter 6, section on theoretical and policy implications).

Seventh, consideration of the consequences of cyclical movements will be limited to the impact of the movement of global cycles on cycles in developing countries. Although it is recognised that such cycles have considerable significance for understanding socio-economic phenomena such as poverty, employment, living standards, welfare expenditures by governments, and the like, these will not be addressed in the present study.

Finally, although the study has certain obvious implications for the development of business cycle indicators (i.e., leading, lagging, and coincident indicators), this book will not touch on this aspect, since it is felt that it would not contribute anything to the core focus of the present study.

This book is organised as follows. The chapter following this introduction will undertake a broad review of the relevant literature on business cycles, with a view to attempting to highlight weaknesses of existing theories with a view to developing an alternative approach. Particular emphasis is placed on what is seen as the mistaken conceptualisations of cycles in the standard mainstream literature and how these tend to inform methods used for the identification of cycles and the explanation of their drivers. As was indicated above, the relevant literature is that pertaining to the general conception of generic cycles and their identification as well as the drivers of global and developing country cycles. The starting point of the literature review will be conceptions of business cycles. Most attention is paid to mainstream conceptions of generic cycles, since these are of necessity the foundation of conceptualisation of other cycles, viz., global and (sub-global groupings of) developing country cycles. This will be followed by a review of mainstream literature on methods to be used in the identification of cycles, and, by implication, in the establishment of their existence. The literature reviewed spans methods used in the identification of cycles in general, and global and developing country cycles. The final part of the literature review then considers literature on drivers of cycles at the global and developing country cycles. The focus of the literature pertaining to drivers of global cycles is the country drivers of global cycles, and the focus of the literature pertaining to drivers of cycles in developing countries is the extent to which exogenous forces can be considered to be the major drivers of these cycles. Against this backdrop, Chapter 3 will develop an alternative conception of the cycle and method for its identification. The conception of the generic cycle used in the present study will be developed on the basis of a critique of various implicit or explicit conceptualisations of such cycles found in the mainstream literature. The methodology to identify cycles will then be used in Chapter 4 to identify global cycles as well as cycles pertaining to sub-global groupings of countries. Implicit in this methodology is the notion that cycles in clusters of countries need to be understood with reference to the global cycle, being conditioned by the latter. Chapter 5 then attempts to determine the major country drivers of the global cycles and the extent to which the groupings of developing country cycles are driven by forces driving global cycles. It will be shown that the key drivers of the global cycles are not the large economies *per se* but the large manufacturing economies. A clear implication to be derived from the data is the significance of the role of China as one of the most important drivers, if not the major driver, of the global cycle. It will also be shown that the key drivers of cycles in developing countries are external to these economies, as manifest in the importance of trade in the movement of cycles in these countries. An econometric Appendix is added to support the exploratory data findings presented in Chapter 5. The final chapter then draws together the major findings and key contributions of the study, discusses their theoretical and policy implications, and considers the directions in which further research might be developed.

Notes

1 In this book, the terms 'business cycles' and 'economic cycles' are used interchangeably. The term 'cycles' is used as a short form of both of these. 'Business cycles' is the more widely used of the two in the academic literature because business is typically seen as the main driver of the cyclical process. Given that the present book aims to study cycles in general economic activities, such cycles will be referred to as economic cycles.
2 The pioneers in the study of business or economic cycles include William Stanley Jevons and Karl Marx. Important figures in the subsequent development of cycle analyses include Arthur F. Burns, Wesley C. Mitchell, Joseph A. Schumpeter, Jan Tinbergen, and Hyman P. Minsky to name just a few.
3 See, for example, Bernanke (2004).
4 IMF projects the 70% of global economy is expected to slowdown in growth in 2019.
5 Former Chair of the U.S. Federal Reserve, Ben S. Bernanke (2012), stated in a speech of 31 August 2012: "because of various unusual headwinds slowing the recovery, the economy needs more policy support than usual at this stage of the cycle"; for the implementation of monetary policy and forward guidance. Similarly, in a commentary on the state of the U.S. economy, Janet L. Yellen (2015b), stated that: "…because, I noted in my remarks, the recovery from the financial crisis has been very slow. … This [cycle]…may turn out to be a very different cycle than past cycles".
6 These studies have typically focused on the causes of the observed cycles, as well as their frequency and amplitudes.
7 Similarly, for example, Rediker et al. (2016, p. 14) argue in this regard, "[o]ne thing is increasingly certain: China can no longer argue that it is a passive recipient of the policy choices made by others. The impact of Chinese policies are [sic] now felt globally". The financial journalist Ruchir Sharma (2014) also comments "[w]hen the U.S. sneezes, the world catches a cold, an old saying goes. But now it's China's health that matters most".
8 The understanding on global cycles and cycles pertaining to the groupings of countries throughout this book is also relevant to the cycles in individual countries (see more details, Ikeda, 2018).
9 Confusion often arises between the conceptualisation and the analysis of actual cycles in capitalist economies since the former have traditionally been based on the latter; typically on actual cycles in the most advanced economies (viz., the United States in more recent times and the United Kingdom in the early epochs of capitalist development) as generic representatives of capitalist economies (see the further elaboration on this point in Chapter 2, section on conception of cycles).
10 This study will use the terms 'orthodox' and 'mainstream' interchangeably with both referring to a basic adherence to Neoclassical thinking.

11 The major sub-schools of Neoclassicals in areas of the business cycle research in the present study are taken as the real business cycle (RBC) approach, the equilibrium business cycle (EBC) approach, the Monetarist approach, and the Austrian business cycle (ABC) approach.

12 For more details on EDA, see Erickson and Nosanchuk (1979) and NIST/SEMATECH (n.d.).

13 The following statement by Alexander Loveday in his preface to the prominent Nobel prize winning Dutch economist Jan Tinbergen's book on business cycles (1939, p.6) perhaps best captures the alternative thinking to the mainstream view in this regard:

> The system of analysis employed cannot do more than submit preconceived theories to statistical test. The economist, and not statistician, must in the first place indicate what, in the light of logical reasoning from ascertained facts, would appear to be the provable causal relations.

14 See the work by McCloskey (1983) and Ziliak and McCloskey (2008) regarding statistical and economic significance.

15 This is not to say that all those who adopt such empirical methods pay no heed to theory. Jan Tinbergen, who is famed for his pioneering work in the econometric analysis of business cycles, was well aware of the pivotal importance of theory when applying econometric methods.

16 Many perceive the danger of the blind application of results obtained by econometric methods when it comes to understanding the real economy and making policy decisions. For example, former Chair of the Federal Reserve, William McChesney Martin, noted:

> [w]e have fifty econometricians working for us at the Fed.... The danger with these econometricians is that they don't know their own limitations, and they have a far greater sense of confidence in their analyses than I have found to be warranted.... The flaws in these analyses are almost always imbedded in the assumptions upon which they are based. And that is where broader wisdom is required, a wisdom that these mathematicians generally do not have.
>
> (McCormack, 2013, p. 56)

17 For example, the IMF provides quarterly real GDP data for around 80 countries but for a relatively shorter time period than with the annual data, and for relatively fewer developing countries than those covered by the annual data of the World Bank.

18 Although Angus Maddison provides long historical data series on real GDP growth for several countries (Maddison Historical Statistics; see website link in the References), it was decided not to use these data here for the following reasons. First, the country coverage is not as extensive as in the World Bank data which are used. Second, the data only extend up to 2010, and therefore do not cover important post-2010 developments, which point to the increasingly prominent role of the Chinese economy in driving the global economy.

19 Real GDP growth rates are preferred by most analysts to alternative GDP variables such as GDP per capita when studying cyclical movements in the economy; the former is seen as better able to capture the growth dynamics of an economy while the latter are seen as more appropriate for studies of living standards.

20 For the World Bank, "there is no longer a distinction between developing countries (defined in previous editions as low- and middle-income countries) and developed countries (previously high-income countries)" (blog post by Fantom et al., 2016).
21 Schumpeter (1939) proposed the classification of cycles into four generic types depending on their duration and causes. These are: the Kitchen (3–5 years, inventory), the Juglar (7–11 years, fixed investment), Kuznets (10–15 years, infrastructure), and the Kondratieff cycle (40–60 years, structural change, technological advancement etc.).
22 Some have argued that there are five long cycles (see, for example, Mandel, 1995[1980]).
23 Although developments in the FIRE (finance, insurance, and real estate) sector can most certainly be argued to have important consequences for an understanding of cyclical movements in aggregate output (e.g., triggering turning points and aggravating movements in certain of these cycles), these are seen as for the most part of secondary importance given the specific objectives of the study — to provide an understanding of the nature and country drivers of cycles in developing countries.

References

Bernanke, B.S. (2004) 'The great moderation', Remarks by the Governor, at the Meetings of the Eastern Economic Association, *Board of Governors of the Federal Reserve System*, 20 February 2004, Washington D.C., Available at www.federalreserve.gov/boarddocs/speeches/2004/20040220/ [Retrieved 10 April 2017].

Bernanke, B.S. (2012) 'Monetary policy since the onset of the crisis', Speech at the Federal Reserve Bank of Kansas City Economic Symposium, Jackson Hole, Wyoming, *Board of Governors of the Federal Reserve System*, 31 August 2012, Washington D.C., Available at www.federalreserve.gov/newsevents/speech/bernanke20120831a.htm [Retrieved 16 May 2019].

Blanchard, O.J. (2008) 'The state of macro', *National Bureau of Economic Research*, Working paper, No. 14259.

Erickson, B.H. and Nosanchuk, T.A. (1979) *Understanding Data: An Introduction to Exploratory and Confirmatory Data Analysis for Students in the Social Sciences* (Milton Keynes, U.K.: Open University Press).

Fantom, N., Khokhar, T. and Purdie, E. (2016) 'The 2016 edition of world development indicators is out: Three features you won't want to miss', *World Bank*, The DATA blog, 15 June 2019, Available at http://blogs.worldbank.org/opendata/2016-edition-world-development-indicators-out-three-features-you-won-t-want-miss [Retrieved 10 April 2017].

Ikeda, E. (2012) 'The causes of business cycles: An evaluation of mainstream views', *Centre Européen de Recherches Internationales et Stratégiques*, Master's thesis.

Ikeda, E. (2018, September) *Global and Developing Country Business Cycles* (Den Haag: International Institute of Social Studies, Erasmus University Rotterdam), Doctoral dissertation, Available at https://repub.eur.nl/pub/110795 [Retrieved 15 June 2019].

International Monetary Fund. (2019, April) *World Economic Outlook: Growth Slowdown, Precarious Recovery* (Washington, D.C.: International Monetary Fund).

Khokhar, T. and Serajuddin, U. (2015) 'Should we continue to use the term "developing world"?' *World Bank*, The DATA blog, 16 November 2015, Available at http://blogs.worldbank.org/opendata/should-we-continue-use-term-developing-world [Retrieved 15 May 2019].

Krugman, P. (2009) 'How did economists get it so wrong?' *New York Times*, 2 September 2009, Available at www.nytimes.com/2009/09/06/magazine/06Economic-t.html [Retrieved 1 April 2017].

Loveday, A. (1939) 'Preface' in Tinbergen, J. (ed.) *Statistical Testing of Business Cycle Theories: Part II Business Cycles in the United States of America, 1919–1932* (Geneva: League of Nations), pp. 5–7.

Lucas, R.E. Jr. (2003) 'Macroeconomic priorities', *American Economic Review*, 93(1), 1–14.

Mandel, E. (1995[1980]) *Long Waves of Capitalist Development: A Marxist Interpretation* (London: Verso).

McCloskey, D.N. (1983) 'The rhetoric of economics', *Journal of Economic Literature*, 21(2), 481–517.

McCormack, R.T. (2013) *A Conversation with Ambassador Richard T. McCormack* (Arlington: Xlibris).

Nielsen, L. (2011) 'Classifications of countries based on their level of development: How it is done and how it could be done', *International Monetary Fund*, Working paper, WP/11/31.

NIST/SEMATECH. (n.d.) *e-Handbook of Statistical Methods*, Online book, Available at www.itl.nist.gov/div898/handbook/

Rediker, D., Economy, E. and Levi, M. (2016) 'The geo-economic implications of China's changing growth strategy', in *Geo-economics with Chinese Characteristics: How China's Economic Might Is Reshaping the World* (Geneva: World Economic Forum), pp. 13–15. www3.weforum.org/docs/WEF_Geoeconomics_with_Chinese_Characteristics.pdf

Reid, D. (2019) 'IMF's Lagarde says a China slowdown, if fast, would constitute a real risk', *CNBC*, 24 January 2019, Available at www.cnbc.com/2019/01/24/imf-lagarde-china-slowdown-if-fast-real-risk.html [Retrieved 15 May 2019].

Schumpeter, J.A. (1939) *Business Cycles: A Theoretical, Historical and Statistical Analysis of the Capitalist Process*, first edition, Vol I (New York: McGraw-Hill).

Sharma, R. (2014) 'Global markets catch the Chinese flu', *Wall Street Journal*, 14 October 2014, Available at www.wsj.com/articles/ruchir-sharma-global-markets-catch-the-chinese-flu-1413503014 [Retrieved 8 April 2017].

Yellen, J.L. (2015a) 'The outlook for the economy', Speech at the Providence Chamber of Commerce, Providence, Rhode Island, *Board of Governors of the Federal Reserve System*, 22 May 2015, Available at www.federalreserve.gov/newsevents/speech/yellen20150522a.htm [Retrieved 15 May 2019].

Yellen, J.L. (2015b) 'Federal Reserve Chair Janet Yellen says U.S. economy has "recovered substantially" and sees "continued economic growth"', Excerpts from Dr. Yellen's remarks, *The Economic Club of Washington D.C.*, 2 December 2015, Available at www.economicclub.org/sites/default/files/transcripts/Hon.%20Janet%20Yellen%20Economic%20Club%20Transcript.pdf [Retrieved 22 May 2017].

Yellen, J.L. (2016) 'The outlook, uncertainty, and monetary policy', Speech at the Economic Club of New York, New York, *Board of Governors of the Federal Reserve System*, 29 March 2016, Available at www.federalreserve.gov/newsevents/speech/yellen20160329a.htm [Retrieved 15 May 2019].

Ziliak, S.T. and McCloskey, D.N. (2008) *The Cult of Statistical Significance: How the Standard Error Costs us Jobs, Justice, and Lives* (Ann Arbor: University of Michigan Press).

Website

Maddison Historical Statistics. www.rug.nl/ggdc/historicaldevelopment/maddison/

2 Current state of business cycle literature

Introduction

This chapter aims to critically review the existing literature on business cycles to ascertain the current state of knowledge on business cycles, including its shortcomings and gaps, with a view to laying the foundations for the extension of this analysis to the study of cycles at the global level and in developing countries, on particular for the development of a different approach founded on an alternative conceptualisation of cycles in the following chapter. As indicated in Chapter 1, the focus of review will be the mainstream or orthodox Neoclassical literature that dominates the academic literature on business cycles.

The particular concern of this review is the literature pertaining to generic, global, and developing country cycles.[1] The literature considered to be of particular relevance is that on the basic conception of cycles, their identification (establishment of existence), and their drivers. The analysis begins with the conception of cycles because researchers studying business cycles have used—either explicitly or implicitly—a wide variety of conceptualisations, with the particular conceptualisations used conditioning to a large extent the outcomes of their analyses. This is followed by a consideration of the literature on cycle identification which includes an assessment of the data used, variables selected, methodologies applied, and empirical results obtained. The discussion of the generic cycle literature will make use of relevant U.S. data[2] as and when required since these data are typically the most frequently used in studies of such cycles. The last part of the chapter is a consideration of drivers of global and developing country cycles. The focus of the literature on global drivers is limited to that pertaining to the country driver or drivers of global cycles. Particular attention is paid to the literature which looks at whether global cycles are to be understood as driven by the advanced countries *per se*, and especially the United States. The focus of the literature on developing country drivers is on whether cycles in developing countries, if they can be deemed to exist, are driven by internal (domestic) or external forces, especially the global cycles. Again, it will be shown that the answer to this question is very much tied up with the way that cycles are conceptualised in the first place.

Conception of cycles

Most of the literature on conceptualising cycles has tended to focus on generic cycles, with the conceptions of cycles pertaining to individual countries being those of advanced countries, particularly the United States. However, given the particular concerns of the present study, attention needs also to be paid to the conceptualisation of cycles at the global and the developing country levels. Of particular note, throughout much of the following study, is the distinction to be drawn between cycles and fluctuations.

Generic cycles

The review of the literature on cycles needs to begin with the conception of the generic cycle. The conceptualisation of the generic cycle refers to the abstract and general conceptualisation of cycles in capitalist economies without reference to any particular concrete form that it might assume. This is considered to be an important point of departure because such a conceptualisation is seen as the foundation for the understanding of how actual cycles are conceived and explained. This is not to deny that the conception and explanation of generic cycles are informed by observation and analyses of actual cycles. Indeed, it cannot be denied that the general conception of most economic phenomena is based on actual observations, without implying that what is being analysed is the particular phenomenon being observed.[3] In fact, the general practice, irrespective of the particular school of thought, has been to use cycle phenomena in the most advanced economy for this purpose. Hence, early cycle analyses made use of observations and analyses of cycles pertaining to the British economy (see, for example, Marx, 1981) while more recent analyses (those from the mid-20th century onwards) have tended to make use of cycle phenomena pertaining to the U.S. economy. That is to say, the use of data pertaining to actual economies for the conception and analyses of generic cycles should not be taken as implying that what is being conceptualised and analysed is the cycle pertaining to the particular advanced economy rather than the cycle pertaining to capitalist economies *per se*.

The general consensus in the literature is that a business cycle is to be conceived of as an expansion in economic activities followed by a contraction, or *vice versa*. Perhaps one of the best described such conceptualisations of the business cycle is provided by Moore (1961, pp. 45–46):

> … the alternating periods of expanding and contracting economic activity defined as business cycles were characterized by a *system* of relations among different factors or aspects of economic activity… the system as a whole was extremely complex, both from a statistical and an economic point of view.

For the majority of modern scholars, typically mainstream economists, business cycles are best described as random **fluctuations** in economic activities. This conception contains no implication of any periodicity. As a result, the term business 'cycle' is argued by some of these scholars to be a misnomer (see, for example, Prescott, 1986; Zarnowitz, 1992, p. 22; Knoop, 2010). The well-known mainstream economist Robert Lucas (1977, p. 10) is quite explicit in this regard, arguing that 'attempts to document and account for regular cyclical movements need not be connected in any way to a presumption that such movements are an inevitable feature of capitalist economies'. Rather, cycles are seen as the result of shocks that hit the economy in a random manner resulting in its temporary deviation from an equilibrium, full-employment, growth path. Romer (n.d.) explains:

> Just as there is no regularity in the timing of business cycles, there is no reason why cycles have to occur at all.… Business cycles do occur, however, because disturbances to the economy of one sort or another push the economy above or below full employment.

One of the tacit assumptions of the conception of cycles as random fluctuations is that the trend growth of the economy is independent of cyclical movement—there is no 'path dependency' of the trend on the short-run movement in economic growth.[4] Specifically, it is assumed that the cyclical movement of the variable has no bearing on its long-term trend, and the expansion and contraction are defined as relative to the trend movement. Indeed, it is for this reason that the cycle is often referred to as a 'deviation cycle' (see the seminal work by

Mintz, 1969, 1972).[5] These deviation cycles are also known as 'growth cycles'[6] (see further elaboration in section on identification and existence of cycles below).[7]

Evidence provided by organisations such as the National Bureau of Economic Research (NBER) and Economic Cycle Research Institute (ECRI) cast doubt on this notion that the alternating periods of expansions and contractions in economic activity can be seen as non-recurrent, symmetric, and the result of random shocks. The NBER, in particular, provides a considerable amount of evidence for such recurrence, documenting the existence of 33 cycles in the United States since the mid-1850s, with an average periodicity of some four to six years (see NBER, 2010a).[8] The problem for mainstream academics is that the implications to be derived from this type of evidence contradict some basic tenets of their views on how capitalist economies work, such as the notion that these economies are essentially in equilibrium unless disturbed by shocks.

Some mainstream cycle economists do acknowledge the existence of recurrent cycles, even if only tacitly.[9] They typically follow the pioneering work of two U.S. economists, A.F. Burns and W.C. Mitchell, who were in fact largely responsible for the research of the NBER referred to above. On the basis of their research, Burns and Mitchell conceived of the phenomena associated with cycles as recurrent and non-periodic. Their definition is one of the most frequently cited conceptualisations of the business cycle. For Burns and Mitchell (1946, p. 3):

> Business cycles are a type of fluctuation found in the aggregate economic activity of nations that organize their work mainly in business enterprises: a cycle consists of expansions occurring at about the same time in many economic activities, followed by similarly general recessions, contractions, and revivals which merge into the expansion phase of the next cycle; this sequence of changes is recurrent but not periodic; in duration business cycles vary from more than a year to ten or twelve years; they are not divisible into shorter cycles of similar character with amplitudes approximating their own.

This conception of the cycle is referred to in the literature as the 'classical cycle' conception, because of its similarity with the conceptualisations of the Classical economists, such as Karl Marx.[10] For Marx, as for Burns and Mitchell, cycles are recurrent and have no fixed periodicity. Rather, their periodicity holds in a loose sort of way. In fact, for Marx (1969[1865], online archive), 'capitalistic production moves through certain periodical cycles. It moves through a state of quiescence, growing animation, prosperity, overtrade, crisis, and stagnation'. A number of Marxist scholars have understood Marx's conceptualisation of cycles to be distinct from (random) economic fluctuations. In discussion with the Japanese Marxist Samezo Kuruma (1972, online archive) one scholar argued:

> The common expression 'business *fluctuation*' or 'economic *fluctuation*' differs from the term 'business *cycle*.' In the case of 'fluctuation', the emphasis is merely on a change—it could be either an arbitrary change or a necessary or regular one—whereas in the case of 'cycles' we are dealing with a regular expression of this 'fluctuation'.

The classical cycle conception of Burns and Mitchell, unlike the cycle conceptions of Marx and John Maynard Keynes,[11] lacks any underlying theoretical framework explaining why and how cycles can be conceived of as recurrent (and of a fixed periodicity in the case of Keynes). It is this lacuna that allows researchers from the orthodox Neoclassical approach to adopt the conception of cycles of Burns and Mitchell while continuing to adhere to their conceptualisations of capitalist economies as essentially in equilibrium. Specifically, it allows them to implicitly, if not explicitly, conceive of recurrent cycles as the product of repeated, regular and persistent exogenous shocks. The famous Neoclassical mathematical economist, Tjalling Koopmans (1947, p. 172), argued that the work of Burns and Mitchell on cycles amounted to 'measurement without theory' as 'the book [by Burns and Mitchell] is unbendingly empiricist in outlook…'.

One could argue that the lack of clarity with regard to the underlying theoretical framework of Burns and Mitchell stems from its endorsement of one or another form of Marx's and Keynes' conceptualisations of capitalist economies—as inherently unstable, with cycles being the manifestations of the workings of such economies. This notion that cycles are the product of the internal workings of an inherently unstable economic system is something which would have been unacceptable to either Burns or Mitchell at the time of the development of their analytical approach, and even more so to their sponsors at the NBER.[12] It is for this reason, more than any other, that the work of Burns and Mitchell is referred to as 'modern classical cycle' in this research, for the express purpose of differentiating it from that of Classical theorists, especially Marx, and their modern descendants such as Keynes.

Global cycles

It is fair to say that research on the phenomenon of global cycles is sparse, with no explicit conception of such cycles. One reason for this is that, until recently, there appeared to be no evidence supporting the existence of such a phenomenon. The first thing of note about the few studies of global cycles which can be found in the literature is that terms 'global cycles', 'world cycles' and 'international cycles' are often used interchangeably (see, for example, Canova and Dellas, 1993; Cookie et al., 2015). To the extent that global cycles are conceived of, this is in terms of a synchronised movement in economic activity of several countries. For example, according to Canova and Dellas (1993, p. 23), '[t]he term "world" or "international" business cycle refers to the existence of common elements in aggregate cyclical behaviour across countries'. Similarly, Kose et al. (2003a, p. 1216) ask, '[i]s there a *world business cycle*? Recent studies have indeed provided evidence that there are many cross-country links in macroeconomic fluctuations'.

The countries whose co-movement and synchronisation are taken as constituting a global or world cycle are typically the large advanced countries, especially the G7[13] (see, for example, Gregory et al., 1997; Bordo and Helbling, 2003, 2010; Aruoba et al., 2011; Berge, 2012; Bernaji et al., 2012; Diebold and Yilmaz, 2015). A few studies have sought to identify global cycles with the co-movement of larger clusters of countries, including a number of developing countries. However, they have not conceived of these as global cycles as such, in the sense of such cycles having an existence which is independent of their constituent parts (countries) (see, for example, Kose et al., 2003a, 2008a, 2008b; IMF, 2007b). This is not to say that certain economies and clusters of economies do not have a considerable influence on the movement of all other economies.

In all such studies, global cycles are seen as any synchronised, random fluctuations in economic activity in these countries, which are the result of random or persistent shocks. In some studies, the shocks are seen as 'common' shocks (see, for example, Canova and Dellas, 1993; Kose et al., 2008b; Bernaji et al., 2012). In other studies, the shocks are seen as those impacting on one country which are directly and simultaneously transmitted to other countries, with the extent and nature of the transmission depending on relative size and the degree of openness of the countries concerned, often in the form of so-called 'spillover' effects (see Canova and Dellas, 1993; IMF, 2007a). For these studies, the global impulses are seen as emanating from the large advanced economies, or even one economy—the United States. Discussion of this point will be taken up below in considering the literature on the alleged drivers of global cycles.

A further problem with the mainstream approaches to the conceptualisation of global cycles, in addition to those noted above, is their conception of the global economy as **interlinked** rather than **integrated** economies (see also Daly, 1999, for the differentiation of internationalisation and globalisation). Interlinked economies are those whose reproduction is independent of one another, but that enter into trade and capital flow relations with one another. Integrated economies are those whose reproduction processes are essentially dependent on one another. Hence, for mainstream approaches and the existing studies adopting these approaches, global cycles can only be conceived of as non-recurrent, random fluctuations of clusters of interlinked economies, and not as recurrent, synchronised cycles in *all or most of* the countries comprising the global economy, with degrees of synchronisation varying depending on all manner of factors. Indeed, it is this implicit mainstream conceptualisation of capitalist economic systems which has precluded the more extensive study of global cycles as the result of forces emanating from the functioning of the global system itself.

Developing country cycles

Most studies of cycles in individual countries[14] are of advanced economies, particularly the United States, Europe, and Japan, with conceptualisations being the sort of generic conceptualisations noted above. Indeed, the generic conceptualisations of cycles discussed above are for the most part based on the observations of economic activities in the United States (see Burns and Mitchell, 1946; Mintz, 1969; Prescott, 1986). That is to say, whatever the country, cycles are conceived of as random or recurrent fluctuations in economic activity. Studies on the developing countries also follow this trend, with, as in the general case, a few exceptions which take as their point of departure the notion of recurrent fluctuations.

The problem with this prevailing conceptualisation is that no distinctions are drawn between cycles and fluctuations, since any and all fluctuations in economic activity are regarded as constituting cycles. Moreover, differences in characteristics of countries are not taken into account, such as levels of development, structures of production, and the extent and nature of the country's integration into the global economy. The consequence of this is that it leads to the misidentification of cycles and a misunderstanding of their drivers because these countries are seen as somewhat independent of the underlying global cyclical forces. With regard to the former, it leads for example to 'double-bottoms' being mistakenly seen as two separate cycles, and many more cycles being identified for developing than for advanced economies. With regard to the latter, it leads to *ad hoc*, *ex post*, explanations of the drivers of individual cycles.

Identification and existence of cycles

The identification of cycles typically builds on certain implicit or explicit conceptualisations of the cycle, with most approaches being based on the sorts of mainstream conceptualisations referred to above. The aim of this section is to review the mainstream literature on the identification of cycles, with a view to highlighting its shortcomings and drawing implications for the development of a different approach founded on an alternative conceptualisation of the cycle.

Generic cycles

The methods most widely used in the identification of cycles are the growth cycle and the modern classical cycle approaches, with a few adopting the so-called growth rate cycle approach. The differences between these approaches pertain to: the data used; the manner in which these data are transformed; the derivation of the cyclical component of the data series; the identification of turning points in cycles; and the depiction of the nature of the cycles (in particular, duration and amplitude). What follows will be a critical review of these various elements of the methods used with a view to laying the foundations for the construction of an alternative methodology for cycle identification, which is consistent with an alternative conception of the cycle. As noted, most identification methods in the literature are constructed using data on the U.S. economy. The key variable used is real Gross Domestic Product (GDP). Many justifications are provided for its use including the fact that it best captures aggregate economic activity. However, there are a number of well-known problems with this variable which have cast doubt on its usefulness in this regard. These range from the omission of large parts of the economic activity of countries, to outright fraud in surveys and estimates used in the construction of the data (see, for example, Krishnan and Rastello, 2015). These problems are particularly evident in the data of developing countries, which are seen as nowhere near as reliable and comprehensive as for the advanced countries (see Jerven, 2013;[15] Hornby et al., 2017).[16] There have been attempts to overcome some of these problems through the use of GDP proxies such as industrial production, electricity consumption, cement usage, levels of imports, etc., but these can in no way be taken as a substitute for the actual GDP data series (see also, for example, NBER, 2010b; Khan, 2016).[17] Large divergences between the actual series and the proxies as well as the lack of consideration for the economic structure are typically seen as pointing to the need for some caution and circumspection in the interpretation of findings based on these data. These well-known problems with this variable, as well as its unsuitability for capturing turning points, have led some researchers—mostly those identified with the modern classical approach to the study of cycles—to use composites of different variables, such as employment, real income, consumption, investment, savings, and industrial production, instead of using a single variable (see, for example, NBER, 2010b). The problem with the use of various composites, or even proxies of economic activity other than real GDP, is that there is no consensus as to the set of variables or proxies to be used. Even the NBER does 'not have a fixed definition of economic activity' (ibid.). To a large extent, this is of course a result of the above-mentioned absence of an explicit theoretical framework (see also Koopmans, 1947; Kydland and Prescott, 1982). It also warrants noting that for many countries, data on most of the variables used in the NBER composite are, in any case, not available.

There are also divergences among those using real GDP growth for identification. These include its frequency and transformation. With regard to the frequency of the data, some studies use quarterly and monthly data, while others use annual data. For many developing countries, only annual data are available for any appreciable length of time. Perhaps even more problematic, especially when trying to compare and evaluate identification methods, is the vast array of data transformations used. Some approaches, such as the growth cycle and modern classical cycle approaches, use natural logarithms of absolute real GDP (see, for example, Baxter and King, 1995; Hodrick and Prescott, 1997; Harding and Pagan, 2002a). Filters are then applied to make the data stationary, and the latter are smoothed further by the application of moving averages (see, for example, Bry and Boschan, 1971; Hodrick and Prescott, 1997). The growth rate cycle approach uses growth rates of real GDP at constant prices, with these rates smoothed to eliminate noise factors (see Friedman and Schwartz, 1975; Zarnowitz and Ozylidrim, 2006). Smoothing methods can also vary, but, according to Layton and Moore (1989, p. 380), tend to be based on the ratio of the current value of the series to its average during the previous periods (for example, 12 months average for monthly, four quarters average for quarterly) and raised to a certain power depending on the weight to be given to most recent observations (for example, 12/6.5 for monthly and 4/2.5 power for quarterly).

A fundamental problem with the various cyclical identification approaches is the techniques used for separating cyclical from trend components. One of the most popular techniques for this is the application of a filter (see Cooley and Prescott, 1995; Zarnowitz and Ozyildirim, 2006).[18,19] The most commonly and widely used filter is the so-called Hodrick-Prescott (HP) filter, closely followed by the so-called Band-Pass (BP) filter.[20] The HP filter has the following form (Hodrick and Prescott, 1977, p. 3);

$$y_t = c_t + g_t \qquad \text{for } t = 1,\ldots,t$$

$$y_t = \text{Min}\left\{\sum_{t=1}^{T} c_t^2 + \lambda \sum_{t=1}^{T}\left[\left(g_t - g_{t-1}\right)-\left(g_{t-1} - g_{t-2}\right)\right]^2\right\} \tag{2.1}$$

where y_t is a given time series;
g is growth component;
c is cyclical component;
t is time; and
λ is a smoothing parameter.

The first term $\left(c_t^2\right)$ of the above equation expresses $(y_t - g_t)^2$, which is the sum of squared deviations that penalises the cyclical components, and the second term is a multiple of the sum of the squares of the trend component's second differences.

The basic problem with the application of these sorts of filters to separate out the cyclical from the trend components is the value to be ascribed for smoothing of the data. This value is referred to as Lambda or 'λ' in the above equation.[21] In most studies of cycles in the U.S. economy using quarterly data this value is typically set at 1,600, and 6.25 when using annual data (see Hodrick and Prescott, 1997; Ravn and Uhlig, 2002). Yet it is admitted that the value assigned to this variable is somewhat arbitrary and that '[t]here is no single correct way to represent these components' (Cooley and Prescott, 1995, p. 27). The problem this gives rise to is supported by the estimations, using quarterly U.S. growth rate data using different values of Lambda, i.e., 1 and 100,000 together with the standard quarterly value of 1,600. The resulting cycles generated show that the lower the Lambda values the lower the amplitudes of the cycles and the greater their frequencies. Or, to put it another way, the lower the Lambda values, the less the cyclical components are penalised, i.e., the less smooth the cycle.[22]

A corresponding problem with cycle identification for those using the above techniques is the use of resulting cycle peaks and troughs in order to date cycles. Typically, the peak is seen as the point just after which the contraction (and recession) starts, and the trough as the point preceding the expansion phase when an economy gets out of recession and starts to expand again. Obviously, what constitute peaks and troughs in the filtered cycles will depend on the Lambda parameter values used for de-trending the data. Hence, there will be a considerable variation in dating between researchers depending on the values used.

Unlike the growth cycles, those adopting modern classical and growth rate cycle methods do not use trends as points of reference in their identification of cycles, but rather turning points. The main methods used by these approaches are referred to as non-parametric and algorithmic approaches.[23] Probably one of the best known of these approaches is the model-free approach, typically used by the NBER for dating of the U.S. cycles. It is so-called because the decision for identifying cycles is made in the final instance by a consensus of members of a cycle-dating committee. One of the weaknesses of this methodology is its subjective nature, with dates even differing between committee members. As a consequence it is seen as 'neither transparent nor reproducible' (Chauvet and Piger, 2003, p. 47; see also Bry and Boschan, 1971, p. 2). Another weakness of the method is that it is seen as requiring complicated and analytically demanding procedures (see Rand and Tarp, 2002; Male, 2010a).

Two alternative, less subjective and/or analytically demanding model-free approaches to cycle identification are the so-called BB procedure developed by Bry and Boschan (1971, p. 21) and the BBQ (Bry and Boschan Quarterly) algorithm developed by Harding and Pagan (2002a, 2006) based on the work of Bry and Boschan (1971) for quarterly data analysis. Bry and Boschan (1971) aimed to follow and simplify the complex criteria laid down in the model-free approach of NBER by providing a 'simple, robust, as transparent as possible and replicable' algorithmic approach (Harding and Pagan, 2002b, p. 1682). Some approaches combine this method of cycle identification with subjective judgements to remove 'false' turning points (see, for example, Layton and Moore, 1989).

A second major problem with certain of the mainstream methods of cycle identification described above is the imposition of cycle symmetry in the course of their application, specifically the application of filters.[24] In fact, it is recognised in the literature on cycle identification methods that such impositions of cycle symmetry cause the duration of the identified cycle phases to be very different from those identified with methods which do not impose such a symmetry (see also Zarnowitz, 2007). For example, growth cycle methods typically impose such symmetry, while modern classical cycle methods do not, resulting in very different cycle durations identified by each. The estimation of the average duration of different cycle phases for the U.S. economy over the period Q1 1947 to Q1 2019 using the two approaches shows a considerable divergence in the time duration of the identified cycles depending on whether or not the filters used impose symmetry. Thus, the HP filter method which imposes cycle symmetry shows an average cycle duration of 12 quarters from trough to peak and 9 quarters from peak to trough, while the BBQ method which does not impose any symmetry shows an average cycle duration of some 22 quarters and 3 quarters, respectively.

In most identification methods, various *ad hoc* rules are adopted to prevent the identification of pseudo turning points. Thus, in the application of HP and BP filters, a certain time period for cycle duration is set (3–5 or 4–6 years for HP filters, and 6–32 quarters for BP filters—see, for example, Baxter and King, 1995; Cooley and Prescott, 1995), with these time periods changing depending on the countries being studied. The BBQ approach, too, generally imposes various controls, so-called censoring rules, to achieve the same results. One of the most important of these rules is the specification of the duration of cycles. For example, the movement of economic variables in a certain direction needs to be longer than five months or two quarters to constitute a given phase of a cycle, and a minimum of fifteen months or five quarters for the completion of both up and down phases (see Harding and Pagan, 2006). These rules in fact introduce a loose periodicity into the model, which in turn excludes the possibility that cycles might exhibit durations greater or less than those periods. Harding and Pagan (2006, p. 4) have argued that the rules are not always necessarily imposed because their rigidity make it 'much harder to formally analyse the statistics produced'.

It has been recognised in the literature on cycle identification that different approaches give rise to different numbers of cycles identified for the same time period. Zarnowitz (2007, p. 4) notes that in studies of cycles of the U.S. economy between 1948 and 1960, those using the growth cycles approach were found to identify many more cycles than those using the (modern) classical cycle approach. The reason for the large number of cycles identified by the growth cycle approach is its underlying conception of cycles as any alternating sequence of expansionary and contractionary economic activity. The even greater frequency of the identified cycles by the growth rate cycle approach is due additionally (i.e., in addition to the underlying conceptualisation of the cycle as any fluctuation in economic activity) to the use of growth rates—growth rates being more sensitive to all manner of random events (see Zarnowitz and Ozyildirim, 2006). The nature of the problem can also be appreciated through the application of the various cycle methods referred to above to U.S. data for the period Q1 1947 to Q1 2019. What this shows is that, while the application of modern classical cycle methods leads to the identification of 11 cycles over this period, that of the growth cycle approach leads to the identification of 13 cycles,[25] and the growth rate cycle approach to 29 cycles.

It needs to be noted that this identification of frequent cycles contradicts the underlying conception of the economy as fundamentally stable. While shocks could be understood to have a bearing on certain fluctuations in developing countries, since their economic system is unstable and uncertain, it is difficult to make sense of how and why regular fluctuations occur in advanced economies, especially economies as large and developed as the United States. This begs the question whether or not these cycles are inherent to the workings of the system.

A final observation regarding the various mainstream methods of cycle identification is that they seem to be at odds with the implicit conception of cycles underlying their analyses, i.e., cycles as random and non-regular movements in economic activity. Specifically, it is apparent that many of these identification methodologies assume that cycles are recurrent and occurring at regular intervals, notwithstanding the fact that fluctuations/cycles are deemed to emanate from random shocks. For example, in his study of growth cycles in advanced economies, Prescott (1986, p. 10) stated that 'we follow Lucas (1977, p. 9) in defining business cycle phenomena as the recurrent fluctuation of output about trend…'. Similarly, when reviewing fluctuations in the real Gross National Product (GNP) of the U.S. economy in the post-Korean war period, Kydland and Prescott (1990, p. 9) refer to the 'consistent patterns in these numbers as business cycle *regularities*'. In fact, the HP and BP filters which are applied to the data by growth cycle analysts are designed to find a regularity in their occurrence, which also implies their recurrence. Hodrick and Prescott (1997 p. 2) argue that their filter is designed to find 'some interesting regularities'. Similarly, the BP filter is designed to 'extract a specified range of periodicities' (Baxter and King, 1995, p. 3) in the observed variables. In such a system, either deterministic or stochastic regularities in terms of the occurrence of events, including those arising from certain assumed underlying causal relationships, are presupposed. These are so-called event regularities (see Lawson, 1997, 2003; Downward, 2002; Lawson in Hirsch and DesRoches, 2009, pp. 104–5). From the ontological point of view, a number of authors, mostly from the non-mainstream school of thought, have questioned the existence of event regularities of the type implied by growth cycle studies. Tony Lawson (2012, p. 4) has argued that such regularities are usually either '*a prior* constructions or *a posterior* observations' in mathematical modelling.

Global cycles

Compared with generic cycle identification, there is a relative dearth of studies on global cycle identification. Of course, in part, and as mentioned above, there is no consensus regarding the existence of such a phenomenon. To the extent that there are such studies of this phenomenon, the focus tends to be on the synchronisation of several individual country cycles.

Most studies of global (and international) cycles use real GDP data since these data are widely available for all countries. A few studies use other variables including industrial production, consumption, retail sales, etc., attempting to capture the movement of aggregate economic activities as is the case of the NBER's identification of the U.S. cycles (see, for example, Kose et al., 2008b; Aruoba et al., 2011). However, this is not the common practice in studies of global cycles quite simply because these data are not readily available for all countries.

The countries included in global cycle identification studies vary across studies in terms of number, geographic coverage and nature of the countries included (see, for example, Gregory et al., 1997; Kose et al., 2003a; 2008a, b; Aruoba et al., 2011; Berge, 2012; Bernaji et al., 2012; Diebold and Yilmaz, 2015). The number of countries ranges from a few to around 100. The majority of studies typically include one or more of the G7 economies in their analysis and largely neglect developing countries. Where developing countries are brought into the analysis, they are for the most part what are referred to as middle-income developing countries. Little or no attention is paid to the particular characteristics of the countries included in the analyses.

The majority of studies typically use non-aggregated data for each country. Very few studies develop composite series, and where they do, these are typically weighted series with weights based on GDP at market prices or purchasing power parities. As in the case of generic cycles, cycles are typically identified through the construction of trends or the derivation of cycle turning points (see, for example, Bordo and Helbling, 2003).

What is readily apparent is that the methodologies adopted to identify global (and international) cycles are, as with generic cycles, quite varied. They can be classified into the following four types. The first, and the simplest, identification method of global cycles is the level of growth rates in composited series. The cycle dates, especially global contractions, are defined relative to a certain threshold of the growth rates, with the most widely used threshold level being 3% (see IMF, 2002; The Economist, 2008; Davis, 2009).[26]

A second identification method, and one favoured by increasing numbers of researchers, uses econometric models to identify the cycle. Particular favourites among such models are the factor models, including the dynamic factor model and Bayesian dynamic latent factor model (see, for example, Gregory et al., 1997; Kose et al., 2008b).[27]

A third identification method involves the discovery of synchronised turning points across several countries. This is, obviously, an extension of the modern classical cycle identification approach using the HP and BP filters and BB/BBQ methods. One of the most extensive studies of the global cycle using this method is by Bernaji et al. (2012). This study attempted to establish ‘world synchronised’ business cycle dates by identifying cycle turning points in aggregated data series pertaining to a cluster of countries, and in a single series in a form of a composite index—the so-called world coincident index. Another similar identification method, which also attempts to identify synchronised cycles by identifying turning points, makes use of a so-called concordance index. Although this method does not formally claim to be identifying global cycles, it is widely used to establish the degree of synchronised movements of similar variables in different countries (see Harding and Pagan, 2002a, p. 370; Nadal-De Simone, 2002; Bordo and Helbling, 2003; Moneta and Rüffer, 2006). In this regard, it is similar to the well-known Pearson correlation contingent coefficient.

A fourth methodology, which also does not purport to identify a global cycle, but does attempt to identify cyclical co-movements between countries, is one which uses correlations (see, for example, Baxter and Stockman, 1989; Backus et al., 1992; Bergman et al., 1998; Agénor et al., 2000; Heathcore and Perri, 2002; Rand and Tarp, 2002; Bordo and Helbling, 2010). Correlations can be regarded as positive and negative, and sometimes expressed as pro-cyclical/synchronised (and positive when the movement is together), countercyclical/decoupling (and negative when the variables move in opposite directions) and a-cyclical (when there is no correlation).

What emerges from these studies is a general consensus that global cycles, at least in the sense of synchronised movements of countries, do exist (see, for example, Gregory et al., 1997; Bordo and Helbling, 2003, 2010; Aruoba et al., 2011). However, the majority of studies see major fluctuations in the extent of synchronised movements between countries, especially among the advanced countries (see, for example, Kose et al., 2008a; Mumtaz et al., 2011).[28] In addition, those studies that identify the existence of global cycles generally tend to focus their studies on the co-movement of advanced country economies. Indeed, when it comes to developing countries, there is generally no consensus regarding their synchronised movement with other countries, even the advanced countries. Thus, while Agénor et al. (2000) and Male (2010a) conclude that advanced and developing country cycles move in a near synchronised way, Kose et al. (2003b, 2008a) suggest that they are largely independent of one another (see also Du Plessis, 2006; He and Liao, 2012; Poměnková et al., 2014). There are also mixed results for movements of developing countries in certain regions. A number of studies deny any synchronised movement of countries in the Latin American region (see, for example, Mejía-Reyes, 2000; Aiolfi et al., 2006), while a number of studies suggest the existence of synchronisation in the East Asian region[29] (see, for example, Moneta and Rüffer, 2006; Imbs, 2011). There are several obvious reasons for the different results obtained by different studies. Aruoba et al. (2011, p. 7) note some of these, including 'country coverage, sample periods, aggregation methods used to create country groups, and econometric methods employed in the case of advanced countries studies'. Another important reason could be the different aims of the research. Most of the studies in which synchronisation is analysed are not fundamentally about synchronisation, but about the explanation of other phenomena, including the transmission of economic impulses between countries.

Many of the problems with the methods used for the identification of global cycles are the same as those noted with regard to their use in the identification of generic cycles. There are, however, additional problems with these methods which merit mentioning. First, many studies use only limited numbers of countries in their analyses and give weight to the largest of these in their samples. Second, there is a marked absence of the use of composite data series. The use of the latter is important because it suggests that the phenomenon being studied is one of an integrated whole. For example, if a global cycle can indeed be deemed to exist such that the economies of all or most countries comprising the global system move in the same direction at the same time, this should be evident from the movement of an appropriately constructed composite indicator, such as the non-weighted real growth of all economies comprising the global system. Third, there appears to be no strong association between the underlying conception of global cycles and the methodology used for their identification, in much the same way as is the case with generic cycles. That is to say, the empirical methods used to identify global (or international) cycles assume the synchronised cyclical movements of countries and the recurrence of this movement, even though the implicit view of cycles underlying most of these analyses is that cycles are the product of random, country-specific shocks. Fourth, the methodologies do not allow for structural change in the global economy over time.

There are also a number of specific problems with the preceding methods which need to be noted here. First, with regard to the simple growth rate approach, there appears to be no theoretical justification for the use of 3% as the threshold rate. A number of authors have pointed to the arbitrariness of this type of approach and questioned the identification results based on it (see Bernaji et al., 2012). Second, the econometric approach makes cycle identification insensitive to structural changes in the global economy and shifts in the relative size and economic power of the countries included in the analyses. Third, the problems associated with the identification of turning points in generic cycles emanating from the different Lambda values used are compounded when it comes to global cycles, since the countries that are included in what is perceived to be the global economy also vary quite considerably between researchers. Lastly, the use of correlation coefficients in the identification of the synchronised movements of countries over short periods of time needs to be handled with a certain degree of caution since they tend to be very sensitive to short- and medium-term deviations between series (see Gayer, 2007).

Developing country cycles

Those studies that seek to identify cycles in individual developing countries typically adopt one or other of the approaches and corresponding methodologies discussed with regard to the identification of the generic cycle. The most common of these are the growth cycle and modern classical cycle approaches and their corresponding methodologies to identify cycles, viz., the HP/BP filters and BB/BBQ approaches, respectively.

The data used for the identification in most individual country cycle studies are real GDP. A few studies have used other measures of real economic activity such as those used by the NBER and others proxies for GDP such as industrial production (see, for example, Agénor et al., 2000; Du Plessis, 2006; Male, 2010b; Calderón and Fuentes, 2011). The justification for use of industrial production comes from the fact that countries which have a proportionately larger agricultural sector tend to have more volatile movements in their GDP due to the influence of exogenous factors such as weather on the growth of these sectors, thus distorting the cyclical picture which emerges from using GDP (see also Rand and Tarp, 2002; Male, 2010a). Some studies which use real GDP also use other variables as a sort of check on the tendencies depicted by trends in real GDP. These other variables include consumption expenditure, industrial production, net exports, interest rates, the trade balance, etc. (see, for example, Stockman, 1990; Agénor et al., 2000; Rand and Tarp, 2002; Neumeyer and Perri, 2005; Dabla-Norris et al., 2010).

The number of developing countries chosen for cycle identification varies between studies. Most studies cover less than half of developing countries. The criterion for the selection of countries to be studied is primarily the availability and quality of data. Additional criteria include, for example, size, income level, openness, stability and investability (see Agénor et al., 2000; Moneta and Rüffer, 2006; Aguiar and Gopinath, 2007; Calderón, 2007). As a consequence, country and regional coverage is far from balanced, with countries from the Asian and Latin American regions featuring most prominently in cycle studies of developing countries. In recent years, there have been increasing attempts to include developing countries from other regions in cycle studies (see, for example, Kose et al., 2003b; Kose and Prasad, 2010; Cashin et al., 2012 for countries in Middle East and North Africa region (MENA)). It is also apparent, as noted earlier, that most studies focus on middle- and high-income, as well as more industrialised, countries with the presumption being that cycles exist in these countries. It is noteworthy that studies on developing countries often exclude large, important developing economies, such as China and Russia, due to availability of data and perceptions that these economies do not behave like normal market economies. One problem with the nature of the coverage of countries in cycle studies of developing countries is the perception that those chosen can be seen as representative of all developing countries, or at least those found in a given region (see, for example, the title of the study by Aguiar and Gopinath, 2007).

In the literature on the nature of cycles in developing countries, most attention is paid to the amplitude or volatility of cycles, i.e., the deviation from the trend after the shocks has been deemed to have hit the system.[30] The amplitude of cycles is generally obtained by the different methodologies related to the identification approach. For those adopting a growth cycle approach, the standard practice is the application of filters and the computation of the standard deviations for the resulting data (see, for example, Agénor et al., 2000; Rand and Tarp, 2002; Aguiar and Gopinath, 2007) or the application of various statistical methods to analyse the raw data directly (see, for example, Kose et al., 2003a, 2003b;[31] Neumeyer and Perri, 2005). Amongst those following the modern classical cycle approach, some make use of the concordance index referred to above, which measures the change in economic activity in complete cycles—see Du Plessis (2006) and Male (2010a)—while others take the difference between phases—trough (peak) to peak (trough)—Calderón and Fuentes (2011)—to identify cycles.

Regardless of differences between studies in terms of the choice of countries, time periods and variables, most growth cycle studies find that cycles in developing countries are more volatile than in advanced countries (see Agénor et al, 2000; Cashin, 2004; Neumeyer and Perri, 2005; Aiolfi et al., 2006; Du Plessis, 2006; Male, 2010a). A number of studies have also found that volatility of some developing countries has declined as they have become more integrated into the global economy. For example, the study by Kose et al. (2003a) found that, for the period 1986–2002, the volatility of a number of developing countries in terms of output, investment, and consumption declined as a result of their increased integration into the global economy. A few studies also point to regional differences. Male (2010a), for example, shows that the amplitude of cycles in Asian countries during the expansion phase is greater than in other regions, and their contractions relatively smaller, while Calderón and Fuentes (2011) show the contractions in Asian countries to be greater than in Eastern Europe and Latin America.

One problem shared by all studies is with respect to the quality and availability of the requisite data—hence the tendency of some researchers to substitute industrial production for GDP data. However, there are good reasons to doubt whether industrial production reflects aggregate economic activity (see NBER, 2010b). Moreover, there is a tendency for those researchers using industrial production to choose more industrialised developing countries to test for the existence of cycles, thereby biasing their sample and distorting the general findings of their research on developing countries.

Another problem which afflicts most of the studies seeking to identify cycles in developing countries is that little or no attention is paid to distinctions between these countries in terms of their structures of production, viz., the extent of their dependence on agriculture, services, raw material production, and the like. In this context, a number of researchers studying the nature of cycles in developing countries tend to give the impression that the results of their studies of a selection of developing countries are applicable to all developing countries without qualification.[32]

In identification studies using HP and/or BP filters, little or no attention is paid to the derivation of the appropriate parameter value for the de-trending of the data, say with reference to the particular characteristics of the developing country being studied, and changes in these characteristics over time. As a result, the entire cycle identification exercise looks suspiciously like a data-fitting exercise, especially given the absence of a reference cycle. Moreover, it is not often recognised in studies using these filters that the choice of one or other filter biases the identification results in one direction or another. Specifically, the use of the HP filter biases the identification results in favour of high volatility, while the BP filter does the opposite. Thus, as Agénor et al. (2000) explain, the use of the HP filter gives rise to higher cycle amplitudes because it tends to eliminate low-frequency cycle variations, and, since the BP filter takes out high-frequency cycle variations, the estimated volatility it gives rise to is smaller than that of the HP filter.

A major problem with the application of the BB/BBQ method in the identification of cycles in developing countries is that it causes analysts to miss cycles in those developing countries which are experiencing rapid economic growth, and/or to mistake fluctuations for cycles in these countries. The source of the problem is, on the one hand, the use of censoring rules leading to a missing of turning points, and, on the other hand, the absence of any clear-cut criteria for distinguishing between recessions and slowdowns. Du Plessis (2006) recognises these problems and seeks to overcome them by eliminating the trend component in fast-growing economies in the manner of Harding and Pagan (2001). However, as discussed in the generic cycle section, the trend component should be seen as a part of the identification. For the study of the nature of cycles, in particular for the amplitude, due to the censoring rules, the BB/BBQ method rules out smaller than usual movements in cycles (see Zarnowitz, 1991, p. 10). Also, it is apparent that the amplitudes derived will change if the selected turning points are varied. This in turn implies that the identification process (and the definition of cycles underlying this) already conditions findings on the nature of cycles.

In most studies of the nature of cycles in developing countries no explanation is provided for why duration and amplitudes of cycles should be of a certain magnitude, why and how they might change over time, why they would be greater than those in advanced countries and whether (and how) the differentials might change over time. What we are left with is a series of empirical observations with various *ad hoc* explanations attached.

An important omission in approaches used to identify cycles in developing countries is that they pay no heed to the global cycle as the point of reference for their identifications. Indeed, developing country cycles are only identified with reference to an idealised advanced country cycle (see, for example, Agénor et al., 2000; Male, 2010a). This seems at odds with the observed reality of cycles in developing countries being fundamentally conditioned by global forces, albeit largely dominated by advanced countries.

Finally, studies attempting to identify cycles in developing countries, like those attempting to identify generic and global cycles, tend to overlook or disregard their implicit conceptualisations of cycles as the result of random shocks. Thus, many of these studies conceive of the timing, duration, and amplitudes of cycles as similar notwithstanding the fact that they are hypothesised (implicitly or explicitly) as resulting from random shocks.

Drivers of cycles

The focus of this section is particularly the country drivers of global cycles as well as the internal versus external drivers of cycles in developing countries.[33] The existing literature basically accepts the existence of the phenomenon of the global (or international) and developing country cycles for proceeding with this area of the analyses.

Global cycles

Following the general mainstream view of shocks as the drivers of cycles, it should come as no surprise that most studies of global cycles tend to emphasise the role of external shocks (shocks emanating from outside of the system) in generating these cycles.[34] The shock which triggers global cycles is perceived to be either a common shock affecting all countries at the same time and in the same manner, or a specific shock that hits one or several large economies and is then transmitted to the other economies. Most studies accept that globalisation has increased the interconnectivity between countries, and, therefore, the speed of transmission of shocks between countries, with the trade channel being singled out as one of the main transmitters of shocks (see, for example, Frankel and Rose, 1998; Kose et al., 2008b). Indeed, there is an ongoing debate in the literature about whether recent increases/decreases in global trade have had a bearing on the extent and speed of transmission of cycle impulses between countries (see, for example, Krugman, 1991, 1993; Kose and Reizman, 1999).

The majority of studies explain global cycles as resulting from shocks emanating from the advanced economies, especially the United States, and transmitted to other countries via various channels, especially the above-mentioned trade channel. Many studies either find that the global cycle is indeed driven by cycles in the advanced economies, particularly the United States, or simply assume this to be the case. For example, Kose et al. (2003a, p. 1229) find that, 'because the world factor is identified by a positive factor loading for the U.S. output growth, there is a sense in which what is good for the United States is good for the world'. Krugman (2016) also argues that recessions in the United States appear to transmit to other countries, while a number of authors have questioned whether the United States alone can be held responsible for global expansions and contractions in an era when the balance of economic power appears to be shifting away from it (see, for example, Bernaji et al., 2012). What is perhaps even more contentious is the nature of the alleged shocks hitting the advanced economies in the first place. In fact, a wide array of shocks are employed in different studies to explain shocks emanating from the advanced economies and transmitted to the global economy including, for example, productivity, and fiscal and monetary shocks.

One problem with the above explanation of drivers of global cycles is the notion that global cycles, like cycles in general, can be seen as random events. Indeed, the apparent recurrence and certain periodicity of these cycles belie the view that they can be seen as random events, the product of exogenous shocks to the system, whether these are common or emanate from the dominant economies. One consequence of the shocks approach is that it has given rise to all manner of *ex post* explanations of global cycles, without much theoretical rationale or logical consistency in the explanations. Thus, while certain global cycles are attributed to shocks such as major changes in oil prices, similar such shocks occurring at other points in time are (implicitly) seen as not having similar global cycle consequences—but without any explanation being offered as to why. Similarly in the case of shocks allegedly emanating from advanced countries: these are sometimes seen as due to excessive expansions in money stock and at other times as productivity changes or fiscal excesses, without any explanation as to why similar shocks occurring at other periods of time do not generate similar cyclical movements in the economies in question and the global economy.

A further drawback of the shocks approach to the explanation of cycles is that it tends to deter any analysis into the dynamic elements of GDP which drive it. Specifically, it discourages consideration of the importance of industry, and specifically manufacturing, in driving GDP, and, therefore, global manufacturing in driving global GDP. For many non-mainstream economists, manufacturing is of pivotal importance in explaining both the trend and cyclical movement of GDP. A number of these economists take as their point of departure the work of the great Cambridge (U.K.) economist, Nicholas Kaldor. Kaldor developed what has come to be known as Kaldor's growth laws in which he associated rapid economic growth with a rapid growth of the manufacturing sector (Kaldor, 1966; see also Verdoorn, 1949; Thirlwall, 1983, 1986; McCombie, 2006; McCausland and Theodossiou, 2012). The implication of this for understanding the country drivers of global GDP is that emphasis should be placed on the growth of the largest manufacturing producers in the global economy and not simply the largest economies *per se*, although there should be a considerable overlap between the two. It is important to note that although for most countries the service sector accounts for a much larger share of aggregate GDP than manufacturing, this does not mean that this sector is the principal driver of economic growth.[35] Indeed, as Kaldor (1966, 1967) has shown, the contribution of this sector to growth is proportionately much smaller than its relative share of GDP, suggesting that causality runs from manufacturing to service sector growth and not *vice versa*. While this alternative view gives an important theoretical underpinning for the economic growth, it has not been applied to understand the cyclical movements. For those who have linked the economic growth and cyclical movements is notably another non-mainstream economist, Michał Kalecki.

Developing country cycles

It should also cause little surprise to learn that the majority of studies of drivers of cycles in developing countries also focus on shocks as the source of these cycles. Needless to say, there is little or no consensus as to the exact shocks which can be considered to drive the cycle, or even whether these emanate from within or outside of the country in question. Examples of the shocks identified include: productivity shocks

(Kydland and Zarazaga, 2002; García-Cicco et al., 2010), commodity price shocks (Collier and Gunning, 1999), terms of trade shocks (Mendoza, 1995; Hoffmaister and Roldos, 1997; Kose and Reizman, 1999; Broda, 2004), and natural disasters (Hochrainer, 2009). Some authors distinguish between internal (domestic) and external (global or international) shocks, permanent and transient shocks, country- and industry-specific shocks, and real and monetary shocks (see, for example, Chang et al., 2002; Ahmed et al., 2005; Edwards, 2006; Raddatz, 2007; Al-Jawarneh and Sek, 2012).

For shocks to developing countries seen as emanating from the global economy, the emphasis is placed on certain individual, or groupings of, advanced countries, with the transmission channel being for most part the trade channel. Studies emphasising external shocks sometimes refer to domestic cycles as 'imported business cycles' (see Canova and Dellas, 1993). These studies focus on large advanced economies as the main drivers of cycles in the developing countries (see, for example, Dornbusch, 1985; Calvo et al., 1993). As noted above, particular emphasis is placed on the United States as the main driver of cycles in developing countries, and on the various mechanisms by which U.S. cycles are transmitted to the rest of the world, especially developing countries (see Ahmed, 2003; Canova, 2005; Boschi and Girardi, 2008; Burnstein et al., 2008; Comin et al., 2009; Male, 2010a). The reason for the emphasis on the United States is its size, being the largest economy in the world. With the rise of China, an increasing number of studies are focusing on its role as a driver of cycles in developing countries (see, for example, Cesa-Bianchi et al., 2012; Duval et al., 2014). Notwithstanding the above, the majority of studies of cycles in developing countries argue that international and global factors are relatively small in comparison to the domestic factors that drive these cycles (see, for example, Kose et al., 2008b; Al-Jawarneh and Sek, 2012).

As opposed to the mainstream view, there are increasing numbers of studies that attempt to apply Kaldor's growth laws to the developing countries (see, for example, Necmi, 1999; Wells and Thirlwall, 2003; Dasgupta and Singh, 2005; Nicholas, 2005; Storm and Naastepad, 2005). These studies are often associated with extensive discussions of structural changes of the economies, particularly the shift from agriculture towards industry (see, for example, Lewis, 1955; Prebisch, 1984; Lakhera, 2016).

Most research into drivers of cycles in developing countries, like that on their identification, focuses on Asian and Latin American economies (especially Mexico). The selected countries are unevenly distributed, chosen mainly for data availability and the interest of the researchers, as noted above. Given that the majority of studies are undertaken with the primary aim of identifying the transmission channels of cycle impulses from advanced to developing countries, the selection of countries tends to be biased in favour of those which have strong links with the advanced economies of interest.

The methodologies applied for identifying the drivers of developing country cycles are, for the most part, econometric. These include multivariate time-varying models, Vector Auto Regression (VAR) models (including panel and structural VAR), simple OLS models, dynamic factor models, etc. The variables selected for these studies, unlike those for the identification of cycles, differ quite widely, as do, predictably, the time periods chosen.

The first problem with most of the mainstream studies of the drivers of cycles in developing countries is that these drivers are seen as independent of the movement of the global economy. Specifically, while many studies of the drivers of cycles in developing countries point to the importance of the movement of the large economies, such as the United States and, more recently, China, few, if any, pay attention to the movement of the global economy—i.e., to global cycles. This is, of course, in part because of the absence of a concept of the global economy, but also, and more fundamentally, because it militates against the underlying mainstream explanation of cycles—random shocks.

The second problem with studies of the drivers of cycles in developing countries, as the result of shocks, is that this view of drivers is at odds with the methods used for their identification. Specifically, and as noted above, in many cases these methods assume the cycles to be recurrent and not the product of random shocks (see the discussion of cycle identification above). Moreover, while there can be no doubting that the economic dynamism of developing countries is more susceptible to shocks than, say the advanced economies, empirical evidence presented below suggests that these countries experience cyclical patterns of growth independent of those caused by random, country-specific shocks.

The third problem, following from the second, is that the shocks approach makes it difficult to distinguish between domestic and external (shock) drivers of cycles in developing countries. The result is that different studies end up with different menus of drivers of cycles (i.e., the different types of shocks discussed above) which tend to be largely *ad hoc* and dependent on the particular factors deemed important by the individual researcher.

Lastly, while a few studies of the drivers of cycles in developing countries do certainly take into account differences in the characteristics of the developing countries (see, for example, Baxter and Kouparitsas, 2004), most do not. Moreover, those that do take account of differences in the characteristics of developing countries do not see their drivers as fundamentally emanating from the global economy—the global cycle.

Notes

1 For cycles pertaining to clusters of developing countries, absence of literature is covered by the sections on the global and/or developing country cycles.
2 The data were accessed on 16 May 2019. The growth rate data used in this chapter were downloaded from the Federal Reserve Economic Data (FRED) by the U.S. Federal Reserve Bank of St. Louis; the name of the variable is 'Real Gross Domestic Product, Billions of Chained 2012 Dollars, Quarterly, Seasonally Adjusted Annual Rate'.
3 It may, for example, be observed that the founders of both Classical and modern Neoclassical commodity price theory claim to have arrived at their conceptions of how markets work from their empirical observations of how commodity prices are formed and move in various product markets. See, for example, Marx *Capital III* for the Classical approach (Marx, 1981), and Menger (2007[1871]) for the Neoclassical.
4 For more details on the notion of path dependency, see Kaldor (1934), Robinson (1974), and Setterfield (1998).
5 Zarnowitz (1992, p. 232) suggests: '[t]here is much support for the notion that business fluctuations are just random deviations from growth trends'.
6 Although the term 'growth' is frequently seen as pertaining to output growth (i.e., typically real GDP), it is called a 'growth cycle' because of the view of business cycle theorists that '*growth* and *fluctuations* are not distinct phenomena to be studied with separate data and different analytical tools' (Cooley and Prescott, 1995, p. 4; see also Prescott, 1986).
7 Studies on such fluctuations have increased significantly in number and influence over the last 30 years in the area of business cycle studies.
8 In 2012, ECRI recorded 47 cycles in the previous 222 years (see ECRI, 2012).
9 It is widely accepted that there is a regularity in the movements of many macro-economic variables (see, for example, Zarnowitz, 1992).
10 It is often overlooked that Marx is one of the founders of business cycle theory (see Sherman, 1967; Kuruma, 1972).
11 In his study on the trade cycle, Keynes adopts a similar definition and conceptualisation of the cycle to that of Burns and Mitchell, except that he places particular emphasis on 'the regularity of time-sequence and of duration' (Keynes, 1957[1936], p. 313). Subsequent post-Keynesian analyses have tended to discard this aspect of Keynes's cycle conceptualisation and returned to more Classical conceptualisations.
12 There is good reason to believe that this lack of clarity in the conceptualisation of cycles by Burns and Mitchell was the product of a certain amount of political pressure, given the close proximity of both, especially Mitchell, to the U.S. administration (see, for example, Friedman, 2014).

13 These are the United States, Canada, Japan, Germany, France, Italy, and the United Kingdom.
14 Such cycles are referred to as national and/or domestic cycles in the literature.
15 It should be noted, however, that the reliability of data is not only a developing country problem. The business economist John Williams has a website dedicated to questioning basic macroeconomic data provided by the U.S. government and providing alternative data series (John Williams' Shadow Government Statistics: see website link in the References). The problem, as Williams sees it, is the so-called hedonistic data adjustments made by the U.S. authorities.
16 This contains an extensive discussion of the problems with GDP data compiled by the authorities in a number of African countries.
17 The former Chinese premier, Li Keqiang, admitted that the macroeconomic data provided by the Chinese authorities are unreliable, and that he himself relied more on variables such as electricity consumption as a proxy for economic growth. For example, a scandal over data provided by the authorities in Liaoning province further illustrates the problem (see Wildau, 2016).
18 This is also referred to as the 'decomposition' of time series.
19 A similar, though less popular, technique is the so-called phase average trend (PAT) (see Zarnowitz and Ozyildirim, 2006).
20 Variations of these filters are, for example, the so-called Henderson, Kalman, and Blanchard filters.
21 This value penalises the variability in the trend components.
22 See also, 'Figure 2.1 Different parameter value of cycles' in Ikeda (2018).
23 There are, however, other approaches which need to be noted, including parametric approaches such as the Markov-Switching model (see, for example, Hamilton, 1989).
24 To put this into some perspective, it warrants repeating that NBER data and analyses show that cycles are asymmetric and recurrent.
25 Although the peaks and troughs used for cycle identification in the growth and growth rate cycles are subject to debate, changes in the criteria for their identification do not fundamentally alter the conclusions with respect to the differences in numbers of cycles identified by the different approaches.
26 A similar study has been conducted by the UBS (Union Bank of Switzerland), setting the threshold at 2.5% of the growth rates.
27 Variations of the factor model include the dynamic latent factor model (Kose and Prasad, 2010), the generalised dynamic factor model (see Forni et al., 2000), dynamic Markov-Switching model (see Kaufmann, 2000), and the dynamic factor model with time varying parameter (see Del Negro and Otrok, 2008). These are not used for global cycle identification as such but rather the synchronisation between countries and co-movement between variables.
28 See also, for example, Artis and Okubo (2008), Koopman and Azevedo (2008), Afonso and Sequeira (2010), Bordo and Helbling (2010), and Aruoba et al. (2011).
29 They differ in their understanding of the starting period of synchronisation. For example, Imbs (2011) see the spark in Asia only since 2008 Q3.
30 It is worthy of note that researchers on growth cycles rarely refer to the 'amplitude' of cycles.

31 Kose et al. (2003a) do not explain what types of cycle they employ in their study.

32 A few authors have cautioned that country specificity is important for understanding the nature of cycles. For example, Zarnowitz (1991, pp. 8–9) states in this regard that '[t]he nature of business cycles depends on, and changes with, the major characteristics of the economy, society, and polity'.

33 There is a large debate in the existing literature as to whether the cycles are caused by exogenous or endogenous factors. Although this is beyond the scope of the present book (see also Chapter 1), it does recognise the important contributions that have been made by a number of economists in this area, such as Jevons (1878), Frisch (1967[1933]), Tinbergen (1939), Kaldor (1940), Goodwin (1967), Marx (1981), etc.

34 For the general definition, see, for example, Gabisch and Lorenz (1987, p. 77). It is typically said that one of the earliest recognised shocks is climate shock, by William Stanley Jevons.

35 For example, Japan's service sector was around 70% of GDP in 2017 (see World Bank WDI data accessed 15 June 2019), while their macroeconomic policies typically focus on industrial production and currency devaluations to promote manufactured exports.

References

Afonso, A. and Sequeira, A. (2010) 'Revisiting business cycle synchronisation in the European Union', Technical University of Lisbon, Working paper, WP 22/2010/DE/UECE.

Agénor, P.R., McDermott, C.J. and Prasad, E.S. (2000) 'Macroeconomic fluctuations in developing countries: Some stylized facts', *World Bank Economic Review*, 14(2), 251–85.

Aguiar, M. and Gopinath, G. (2007) 'Emerging market business cycles: The cycle is the trend', *Journal of Political Economy*, 115(1), 69–102.

Ahmed, S. (2003) 'Sources of economic fluctuations in Latin America and implications for choice of exchange rate regimes', *Journal of Development Economics*, 72(1), 181–202.

Ahmed, S., Ara, I. and Hyder, K. (2005) 'How external shocks and exchange rate depreciations affect Pakistan? Implications for choice of an exchange rate regime', *MPRA working paper*, No. 16247.

Aiolfi, M., Catão, L. and Timmermann, A. (2006) 'Common factors in Latin America's business cycles', *International Monetary Fund*, Working paper, WP/06/49.

Al-Jawarneh, A. and Sek, S.K. (2012) 'The impact of external shocks on business cycle fluctuation in several developed Asian countries', *Applied Mathematical Sciences*, 6(65), 3209–223.

Artis, M. and Okubo, T. (2008) 'Globalization and business cycle transmission', *University of Manchester*, Discussion paper, No. 110.

Aruoba, S.B., Diebold, F.X., Kose, M.A. and Terrones, M.E. (2011) 'Globalization, the business cycle, and macroeconomic monitoring', *International Monetary Fund*, Working paper, WP/11/25.

Backus, D.K., Kehoe, P.J. and Kydland, F.E. (1992) 'International real business cycles', *Journal of Political Economy*, 100(4), 745–75.

Baxter, M. and King, R.G. (1995) 'Measuring business cycles approximate band-pass filters for economic time series', *National Bureau of Economic Research*, Working paper, No. 5022.

Baxter, M. and Kouparitsas, M.A. (2004) 'Determinants of business cycle comovement: A robust analysis', *Federal Reserve Bank of Chicago*, Working paper, No. 2004–14.

Baxter, M. and Stockman, M.J. (1989) 'Business cycles and the exchange-rate regime: Some international evidence', *Journal of Monetary Economics*, 23(3), 377–400.

Berge, T.J. (2012) 'Has globalization increased the synchronicity of international business cycles?', *Federal Reserve Bank of Kansas City*, Economic Review, Third Quarter, 5–39.

Bergman, U.M., Jonung, L. and Bordo, M.D. (1998) 'Historical evidence on business cycles: The international experience' in Fuhrer, J. and Schuh, S. (eds.) *Beyond Shocks: What Causes Business Cycles?* Federal Reserve Bank of Boston Conference Proceedings, Conference Series No. 42 (Boston: Federal Reserve Bank of Boston), pp. 65–113.

Bernaji, A., Layton, A.P. and Lakshman, A. (2012) 'Dating the "world business cycle"', *Applied Economics*, 44, 2051–63.

Bordo, M.D. and Helbling, T. (2003) 'Have national business cycles become more synchronized?' *National Bureau of Economic Research*, Working paper, No. 10130.

Bordo, M.D. and Helbling, T. (2010) 'International business cycles synchronization in historical perspective' *National Bureau of Economic Research*, Working paper, No. 16103.

Boschi, M. and Girardi, A. (2008, October) 'The contribution of domestic, regional and international factors to Latin America's business cycle', *Australian National University*, CAMA Working paper, No. 33.

Broda, C. (2004) 'Terms of trade and exchange rate regime in developing countries', *Journal of International Economics*, 63, 31–58.

Bry, G. and Boschan, C. (1971) *Cyclical Analysis of Time Series: Selected Procedures and Computer Programs* (New York: National Bureau of Economic Research).

Burns, A.F. and Mitchell, W.C. (1946) *Measuring Business Cycles* (New York: National Bureau of Economic Research).

Burnstein, A., Kurz, C. and Tesar, L. (2008) 'Trade, production sharing, and the international transmission of business cycles', *Journal of Monetary Economics*, 55, 775–95.

Calderón, C. (2007) 'Trade, specialization and cycle synchronization: Explaining output comovement between Latin America, China and India', *World Bank*, Working paper, No. 66621.

Calderón, C. and Fuentes, J.R. (2011) 'Characterizing the business cycles of emerging economies', *Instituto de Economia*, Second version, No. 371.

Calvo, G.A., Leiderman, L., and Reinhart, C.M. (1993) 'Capital inflows and real exchange rate appreciation in Latin America: The role of external factors', *International Monetary Fund*, Staff papers, 40(1), 108–51.

Canova, F. (2005) 'The transmission of U.S. shocks to Latin data', *Journal of Applied Econometrics*, 20, 229–51.

Canova, F. and Dellas, H. (1993) 'Trade interdependence and the international business cycle', *Journal of International Economics*, 34, 23–47.

Cashin, P. (2004) 'Caribbean business cycles', *International Monetary Fund*, Working paper, WP/04/136.

Cashin, P., Mohaddes, K. and Raissi, M. (2012) 'The global impact of the systemic economies and MENA business cycles', *International Monetary Fund*, Working paper, WP/12/255.

Cesa-Bianchi, A., Pesaran, M.H., Rebucci, A. and Zu, T.T. (2012) 'China's emergence in the world economy and business cycles in Latin America', *Bank of Canada*, Working paper, 2012-32.

Chang, K., Filer, L. and Ying, Y.H. (2002) 'A structural decomposition of business cycles in Taiwan', *China Economic Review*, 13(1), 53–64.

Chauvet, M. and Piger, J.M. (2003, March/April) 'Identifying business cycle turning points in real time', *The Federal Reserve Bank of St. Louis*, 85(2), 47–62.

Collier, P. and Gunning, J.W. (1999) *Trade Shocks in Developing Countries*, Vol 1 (Oxford, U.K.: Oxford University Press).

Comin, D.A., Loayza, N., Pasha, F. and Serven, L. (2009) 'Medium term business cycles in developing countries', *NBER*, Working paper, No. 15428.

Cookie, D.A., Kose, M.A., Otrok, C. and Owyang, M.T. (2015, April) 'Regional vs. global: How are countries' business cycles moving together these days?' *The Regional Economist*, pp. 5–9.

Cooley, T.F. and Prescott, E.C. (1995) 'Economic growth and business cycles' in Cooley, T.F. (ed.) *Frontiers of Business Cycle Research* (Princeton, NJ: Princeton University Press), Chapter 1, pp. 1–38.

Dabla-Norris, E., Minoiu, C. and Zanna, L.-F. (2010) 'Business cycle fluctuations, large shocks, and development aid: New evidence', *International Monetary Fund*, Working paper, WP/10/240.

Daly, H.E. (1999) 'Globalization versus internationalization – Some implications', *Ecological Economics*, 31, 31–37.

Dasgupta, S. and Singh, A. (2005) 'Will service be the new engine of Indian economic growth?' *Development and Change*, 36(6), 1035–57.

Davis, B. (2009) 'What's a global recession?' *Wall Street Journal*, 22 April 2009, Available at https://blogs.wsj.com/economics/2009/04/22/whats-a-global-recession/ [Retrieved 1 June 2019].

Del Negro, M. and Otrok, C. (2008, May) 'Dynamic factor models with time-varying parameters: Measuring changes in international business cycles', *Federal Reserve Bank of New York*, Staff report, No. 326.

Diebold, F.X. and Yilmaz, K. (2015) 'Measuring the dynamics of global business cycle connectedness' in Koopman, S.J. and Shephard, N. (eds.)

Unobserved Components and Time Series Econometrics: Essays in Honor of Andrew C. Harvey (Oxford, U.K.: Oxford University Press), pp. 45–89.

Dornbusch, R. (1985) 'Policy and performance links between LDC debtors and industrial nations', *Brookings Papers on Economic Activity*, 2, 303–56.

Downward, P. (2002) 'Realism, econometrics and Post Keynesian economics' in Dow, C.S. and Hillard, J. (eds.) *Post Keynesian Econometrics, Microeconomics and the Theory of the Firm: Beyond Keynes*, Vol 1 (Cheltenham: Edward Elgar), pp. 481–500.

Du Plessis, S.A. (2006) 'Business cycles in emerging market economies: A new view of the stylised facts', *University of Stellenbosch*, Stellenbosch Economic Working papers, 2/2006.

Duval, R., Cheng, K., Oh, K.H, Saraf, R. and Seneviratne, D. (2014) 'Trade integration and business cycle synchronisation: A reappraisal with focus on Asia', *International Monetary Fund*, Working paper, WP/14/52.

Economic Cycle Research Institute. (2012) 'Revoking recession: 48th time's the charm?' 9 May 2012, Available at www.businesscycle.com/ecri-news-events/news-details/economic-cycle-research-recession-call [Retrieved 1 June 2019].

The Economist. (2008) 'The global slumpometer', *The Economist*, 6 November 2008, Available at www.economist.com/node/12553076 [Retrieved 1 June 2019].

Edwards, S. (2006) 'Monetary unions, external shocks and economic performance: A Latin American perspective', *International Economics and Economic Policy*, 3, 225–47.

Forni, M., Hallin, M., Lippi, M., and Reichlin, L. (2000) 'The generalized dynamic-factor model: Identification and estimation', *Review of Economics and Statistics*, 82(4), 540–54.

Frankel, J. and Rose, A. (1998) 'The endogeneity of the optimum currency area criteria', *Economic Journal*, 108(449), 1009–25.

Friedman, W.A. (2014) *Fortune Tellers: The Story of America's First Economic Forecasters* (Princeton, NJ: Princeton University Press).

Friedman, M. and Schwartz, A.J. (1975) 'Money and business cycle', in *The State of Monetary Economics* (New York: Arno Press), pp. 32–78. www.nber.org/chapters/c5176.pdf, www.nber.org/books/univ65-1

Frisch, R. (1967[1933]) 'Propagation problems and impulse problems in dynamic economics' in *Economic Essays in Honour of Gustav Cassel*, second edition (London: Frank Cass, George Allen & Unwin), pp. 171–205, reprinted. https://books.google.co.jp/books?id=Xb2IYc28X4MC&pg=PP1&source=kp_read_button&redir_esc=y#v=onepage&q&f=false

Gabisch, G. and Lorenz, H.W. (1987) *Business Cycle Theory: A Survey of Methods and Concepts* (New York: Springer-Verlag).

García-Cicco, J., Pancrazi, R. and Uribe, M. (2010) 'Real business cycles in emerging countries?' *American Economic Review*, 100, 2510–31.

Gayer, C. (2007, September) 'A fresh look at business cycle synchronisation in the euro area', *European Commission*, Economic papers, No. 287.

Goodwin, R.M. (1967) 'A growth cycle' in Feinstein, C.H. (ed.) *Socialism, Capitalism and Economic Growth: Essays presented to Maurice Dobb* (Cambridge, U.K.: Cambridge University Press), pp. 54–58.

Gregory, A.W., Head, A.C. and Raynauld, J. (1997) 'Measuring world business cycles', *International Economic Review*, 38(3), 677–701.

Hamilton, J.D. (1989) 'A new approach to the economic analysis of nonstationary time series and the business cycle', *Econometrica*, 57(2), 357–84.

Harding, D. and Pagan, A. (2001) 'Extracting, using and analysing cyclical information', *MPRA*, 15.

Harding, D. and Pagan, A. (2002a) 'Dissecting the cycle: A methodological investigation', *Journal of Monetary Economics*, 49, 365–81.

Harding, D. and Pagan, A. (2002b) 'A comparison of two business cycle dating methods', *Journal of Economic Dynamics and Control*, 27, 1681–90.

Harding, D. and Pagan, A. (2006, June) 'Measurement of business cycles', *University of Melbourne*, Research paper, No. 966.

He, D. and Liao, W. (2012) 'Asian business cycle synchronization', *Pacific Economic Review*, 17(1), 106–35.

Heathcore, J. and Perri, F. (2002) 'Financial globalization and real regionalization', *National Bureau of Economic Research*, Working paper, No. 9292.

Hirsch, C. and DesRoches, C.T. (2009, Summer) 'Cambridge social ontology: An interview with Tony Lawson', *Erasmus Journal for Philosophy and Economics*, 2(1), 100–22.

Hochrainer, S. (2009) 'Assessing the macroeconomic impacts of natural disasters: Are there any?' *World Bank*, Policy Research Working Paper, 4968.

Hodrick, R.J. and Prescott, E.C. (1997) 'Postwar U.S. business cycles: An empirical investigation', *Journal of Money, Credit and Banking*, 29(1), 1–16.

Hoffmaister, A.W. and Roldos, J.E. (1997) 'Are business cycles different in Asia and Latin America?' *International Monetary Fund*, Working paper, WP/97/9.

Hornby, L., Zhang, A. and Pong, J. (2017) 'Fake China data: Was it just one province?' *Financial Times*, 13 March 2017, Available at www.ft.com/content/a5bf42e2-03cf-11e7-ace0-1ce02ef0def9 [Retrieved 10 April 2017].

Ikeda, E. (2018, September) *Global and Developing Country Business Cycles* (Den Haag: International Institute of Social Studies, Erasmus University Rotterdam), Doctoral dissertation, Available at https://repub.eur.nl/pub/110795 [Retrieved 15 June 2019].

Imbs, J. (2011) 'What happened to the East Asian business cycle?' in Devereux, M., Lane, P.R., Park, C.Y. and Wei, S.J. (eds.) *The Dynamics of Asian Financial Integration* (Abingdon: Routledge), pp. 284–310.

International Monetary Fund. (2002, April) *World Economic Outlook: Recessions and Recoveries* (Washington, D.C.: International Monetary Fund).

International Monetary Fund. (2007a, April) *World Economic Outlook: Spillovers and Cycles in the Global Economy* (Washington, D.C.: International Monetary Fund).

International Monetary Fund. (2007b, October) 'Chapter 5: The changing dynamics of the global business cycles', *World Economic Outlook: Globalization and Inequality* (Washington, D.C.: International Monetary Fund).

Jerven, M. (2013) *Poor Numbers: How We Are Misled by African Development Statistics and What To Do About It* (Ithaca: Cornell University Press).

Jevons, W.S. (1878) 'Commercial crises and sun-spots', *Nature*, 19(472), 33–37.

Kaldor, N. (1934) 'A classificatory note on the determinateness of equilibrium', *Review of Economic Studies*, 1(2), 122–36.

Kaldor, N. (1940) 'A model of the trade cycle', *Economic Journal*, 50(197), 78–92.

Kaldor, N. (1966) *Cases of the Slow Rate of Economic Growth of the United Kingdom* (Cambridge, U.K.: Cambridge University Press).

Kaldor, N. (1967) *Strategic Factors in Economic Development* (Ithaca: Cornell University).

Kaufmann, S. (2000) 'Measuring business cycles with a dynamic Markov switching factor model: An assessment using Bayesian simulation methods', *Econometrics Journal*, 3(1), 39–65.

Keynes, J.M. (1957[1936]) *The General Theory of Employment, Interest and Money* (London: Macmillan).

Khan, M. (2016) 'The truth behind China's manipulated economic numbers', *Telegraph*, 19 January 2016, Available at www.telegraph.co.uk/finance/economics/11930766/The-truth-behind-Chinas-manipulated-economic-numbers.html [Retrieved 1 June 2019].

Knoop, T.A. (2010) *Recessions and Depressions: Understanding Business Cycles*, second edition (Santa Barbara: ABC CLIO).

Koopman, S.J. and Azevedo, J.V.E. (2008) 'Measuring synchronization and convergence of business cycles for the Euro area, UK and US', *Oxford Bulletin of Economics and Statistics*, 70(1), 23–51.

Koopmans, T.J. (1947) 'Measurement without theory', *Review of Economic Statistics*, 29(3), 161–72.

Kose, M.A., Otrok, C. and Whiteman, C.H. (2003a) 'International business cycles: World, region, and country-specific factors', *American Economic Review*, 93(4), 1216–39.

Kose, M.A., Otrok, C. and Prasad, E.S. (2008a) 'Global business cycles: Convergence or decoupling?' *Deutsche Bundesbank*, Discussion paper, Series 1: Economic Studies, No. 17.

Kose, M.A., Otrok, C. and Whiteman, C.H. (2008b) 'Understanding the evolution of world business cycles', *Journal of International Economics*, 75(1), 110–30.

Kose, M.A. and Prasad, E.S. (2010, October) 'Resilience of emerging market economies to economic and financial developments in advanced economies', *European Commission*, Economic papers, No. 411.

Kose, M.A., Prasad, E.S. and Terrones, M.E. (2003b, May) 'How does globalization affect the synchronization of business cycles?' *International Monetary Fund*, AEA papers and proceedings, pp. 57–62.

Kose, M.A. and Reizman, R. (1999) 'Trade shocks and macroeconomic fluctuations in Africa', *Journal of Development Economics*, 65(1), 55–80.

Krishnan, U. and Rastello, S. (2015) 'India economy data changes boost growth rate before Modi budget', *Bloomberg*, 30 January 2015, Available at www.bloomberg.com/news/articles/2015-01-30/india-economy-data-changes-boost-growth-rate-before-modi-budget [Retrieved 1 June 2019].

Krugman, P. (1991) 'Increasing returns and economic geography', *Journal of Political Economy*, 99(3), 483–99.

Krugman, P. (1993) 'Lessons of Massachusetts for EMU' in Torres, F. and Giavazzi, F. (eds.) *Adjustment and Growth in the European Monetary Union* (Cambridge, U.K.: Cambridge University Press), pp. 241–61.

Krugman, P. (2016) 'The economic fallout', *New York Times*, 11 November 2016, Available at www.nytimes.com/interactive/projects/cp/opinion/election-night-2016/paul-krugman-the-economic-fallout [Retrieved 1 June 2019].

Kuruma, S. (1972) 'Discussion of Marx's theory of crisis (part 1)', *Marx-Lexikon Zur Politischen Ökonomie Vol 6*, Translated by Schauerte, M., Online archive, Available at www.marxists.org/archive/kuruma/crisis-discussion1.htm [Retrieved 1 June 2019].

Kydland, F.E and Prescott, E.C. (1982) 'Time to build and aggregate fluctuations', *Econometrica*, 50(6), 1345–70.

Kydland, F.E and Prescott, E.C. (1990, Spring) 'Business cycles: Real facts and a monetary myth', *Federal Reserve Bank of Minneapolis*, Quarterly Review, 14(2), 3–18.

Kydland, F.E and Zarazaga, C.E.J.E.M. (2002) 'Argentina's lost decade', *Review of Economic Dynamics*, 5, 152–65.

Lakhera, M.L. (2016) *Economic Growth in Developing Countries: Structural Transformation, Manufacturing and Transport Infrastructure* (Basingstoke: Palgrave Macmillan).

Lawson, T. (1997) *Economics and Reality* (London: Routledge).

Lawson, T. (2003) *Reorienting Economics* (London: Routledge).

Lawson, T. (2012) 'Mathematical modelling and ideology in the economics academy: Competing explanations of the failings of the modern discipline?' *Economic Thought*, 1(1), 3–22.

Layton, A.P. and Moore, G.H. (1989) 'Leading indicators for the service sector', *Journal of Business & Economic Statistics*, 7(3), 379–86.

Lewis, W.A. (1955) *The Theory of Economic Growth* (London: Allen and Unwin).

Lucas, R.E. Jr. (1977) 'Understanding business cycles', *Carnegie-Rochester Conference Series on Public Policy*, 5, 7–29.

Male, R. (2010a, May) 'Developing country business cycles: Characterising the cycle', *University of London*, Working paper, 663.

Male, R. (2010b, May) 'Developing country business cycles: Revisiting the stylised fact', *University of London*, Working paper, 664.

Marx, K. (1969[1865]) 'XIII. Main causes of attempts at raising wages or resisting their fall', in *Value, Price and Profit* (New York: International Co.), online archive, Available at www.marxists.org/archive/marx/works/1865/value-price-profit/ch03.htm#c12

Marx, K. (1981) *Capital: Volume III*, Translated by Fernbach, D. (Harmondsworth: Penguin Books).

McCausland, W.D. and Theodossiou, I. (2012) 'Is manufacturing still the engine of growth?' *Journal of Post Keynesian Economics*, 35(1), 79–92.

McCombie, J.S.L. (2006) 'Kaldor, Nicholas (1908–1986)' in Clark, D.A. (ed.) *The Elgar Companion to Development Studies* (Cheltenham: Edward Elgar), pp. 299–304.

Mejía-Reyes, P. (2000) 'Asymmetries and common cycles in Latin America: Evidence from Markov-Switching Models', *Economía Mexicana Nueva Época*, IX(2), 189–225.

Mendoza, E.G. (1995) 'The terms of trade, the real exchange rate, and economic fluctuations', *International Economic Review*, 36(1), 101–37.

Menger, K. (2007) *Principles of Economics*, Translated by Dingwall, J. and Hpselitz, B.F. (Auburn: Ludwig von Mises Institute), originally published in 1871.

Mintz, I. (1969) *Dating Postwar Business Cycles: Methods and their Application to Western Germany, 1950–1967* (New York: NBER/Columbia University Press).

Mintz, I. (1972) 'Dating American growth cycles' in Zarnowitz, V. (ed.) *Economic Research: Retrospect and Prospect Vol 1: The Business Cycle Today* (New York: NBER/Columbia University Press), pp. 39–88.

Moneta, F. and Rüffer, R. (2006) 'Business cycle integration in East Asia', *European Central Bank*, Working paper series, No. 671.

Moore, G.H. (1961) 'Leading and confirming indicators of general business changes', in Moore, G.H. (ed.) *Business Cycle Indicators, Volume 1: Contributions to the Analysis of Current Business Conditions* (Princeton, NJ: Princeton University Press), pp. 45–109.

Mumtaz, H., Simonelli, S. and Surico, P. (2011) 'International comovements, business cycle and inflation: A historical perspective', *Review of Economic Dynamics*, 14(1), 176–98.

Nadal-De Simone, F. (2002) 'Common and idiosyncratic components in real output: Further international evidence', *International Monetary Fund*, Working paper, WP/02/229.

National Bureau of Economic Research. (2010a) 'US business cycle expansions and contractions', last update 20 September 2010, Available at www.nber.org/cycles.html [Retrieved 1 June 2019].

National Bureau of Economic Research. (2010b) 'The NBER's business cycle dating committee', last update 20 September 2010, Available at www.nber.org/cycles/recessions.html [Retrieved 1 June 2019].

Necmi, S. (1999) 'Kaldor's growth analysis revisited', *Applied Economics*, 31(5), 653–60.

Neumeyer, P.A. and Perri, F. (2005) 'Business cycles in emerging economies: The role of interest rates', *Journal of Monetary Economics*, 52, 345–80.

Nicholas, H. (2005) 'Introduction: Putting industrialization back into development', *Development and Change*, 36(6), 1031–33.

Poměnková, J., Fidrmuc, J. and Korhonen, I. (2014) 'China and the world economy: Wavelet spectrum analysis of business cycles', *Bank of Finland*, Discussion papers, 5.

Prebisch, R. (1984) 'Five stages in my thinking' in Meier, G.M. and Seers, D. (eds.) *Pioneers in Development* (New York: Oxford University Press), pp. 175–91.

Prescott, E.C. (1986, Fall) 'Theory ahead of business cycle measurement', *Federal Reserve Bank of Minneapolis*, Quarterly review, 9–22.

Raddatz, C. (2007) 'Are external shocks responsible for the instability of output in low-income countries?' *Journal of Development Economics*, 84, 155–87.

Rand, J. and Tarp, F. (2002) 'Business cycles in developing countries: Are they different?' *World Development*, 30(12), 2071–88.

Ravn, M.Ø. and Uhlig, H. (2002) 'Notes: On adjusting the Hodrick-Prescott filter for the frequency of observations', *Review of Economics and Statistics*, 84(2), 371–80.

Robinson, J. (1974) *History versus Equilibrium* (London: Thames Polytechnic).

Romer, C.D. (n.d.) 'Business cycles', The concise encyclopaedia of economics, *Library Economics Liberty*, Available at www.econlib.org/library/Enc/BusinessCycles.html [Retrieved 1 June 2019].

Setterfield, M. (1998) 'History versus equilibrium: Nicholas Kaldor on historical time and economic theory', *Cambridge Journal of Economics*, 22(5), 521–37.

Sherman, H.J. (1967) 'Marx and the business cycle', *Science & Society*, A Century of Marx's "Capital", 31(4), 486–504.

Stockman, A.C. (1990) 'International transmission and real business cycle models', *American Economic Review*, 80(2), 134–38.

Storm, S. and Naastepad, C.W.M. (2005) 'Strategic factors in economic development: East Asian industrialization 1950–2003', *Development and Change*, 36(6), 1059–94.

Thirlwall, A.P. (1983) 'A plain man's guide to Kaldor's growth laws', *Journal of Post Keynesian Economics*, 5(3), 345–58.

Thirlwall, A.P. (1986) 'A general model of growth and development on Kaldorian lines', *Oxford Economic Papers*, New series, 38(2), 199–219.

Tinbergen, J. (1939) *Statistical Testing of Business-cycle Theories: 1919–1932. Business cycles in the United States of America*, Vol 2 (Geneva: League of Nations).

Verdoorn, P.J. (1949) 'Fattori che regolano lo sviluppo della produttività del lavoro', L'Industria, 1, 3–10, Translated by Thirlwall, A.P. (1988) 'Factors governing the growth of labour productivity' in Perkins, J.O.N., Van Hoa, T. and Ironmonger, D. (eds.) *National Income and Economic Progress* (London: Macmillan Press), pp. 199–207.

Wells, H. and Thirlwall, A.P. (2003) 'Testing Kaldor's growth laws across the countries of Africa', *African Development Review*, 15(2–3), 89–105.

Wildau, G. (2016) 'China's statistics chief admits some economic data are false', *Financial Times*, 8 December 2016, Available at www.ft.com/content/0361c1a4-bcfe-11e6-8b45-b8b81dd5d080 [Retrieved 2 April 2017].

Zarnowitz, V. (1991) 'What is a business cycle?', *NBER*, Working paper, No. 3863.

Zarnowitz, V. (1992) *Business Cycles: Theory, History, Indicators, and Forecasting* (Chicago: University of Chicago Press).

Zarnowitz, V. (2007, November) 'Persistent business cycles and high economic growth: How to explain their long concurrence in modern capitalism', *Conference Board*, Economics Program Working Paper Series, EPWP #07-03.

Zarnowitz, V. and Ozyildirim, A. (2006) 'Time series decomposition and measurement of business cycles, trends and growth cycles', *Journal of Monetary Economics*, 53, 1717–39.

Website

John Williams' Shadow Government Statistics. www.shadowstats.com/

3 Alternative conceptions and methods of identifying business cycles

Introduction

This chapter aims to develop an alternative (to mainstream) conception of business cycles and a corresponding methodology for their identification. The two must go hand in hand: an alternative conception of cycles demands an alternative methodology for their identification, since the former is implicit in the latter.

The cycles of particular concern in the present chapter are what have been referred to above as generic cycles, global cycles, and cycles pertaining to sub-global groupings of countries, especially developing country clusters.[1] The alternative conceptualisation of generic cycles will provide the basis for the conceptualisation of the other two. The methodology which will be developed with respect to the generic cycles provides the basis for the identification of the global cycles, and in turn provide a basis for the identification of cycles pertaining to clusters of developing countries.

The chapter is divided into two parts. The first part is concerned with the development of alternative conceptualisations of the above-mentioned cycles, while the second part is concerned with the development of an alternative methodology for the identification of these cycles. It warrants repeating that the methodology for the identification of cycles needs to be understood in the context of the prior alternative conceptualisations of cycles.

Developing alternative conceptions of cycles

Generic cycles

The alternative conception of generic business cycles stems from the non-mainstream approach, which was implicit in the criticisms of mainstream Neoclassical conceptions reviewed in Chapter 2. It needs to be emphasised that, notwithstanding these criticisms, the alternative conception of generic cycles uses some elements of existing mainstream Neoclassical conceptions of such cycles which are deemed to be acceptable, and builds on these in a manner which is argued to be consistent with the alternative methods and approach to the study of economic phenomena outlined in Chapter 1.

The alternative conception of generic cycles begins with the core conception of such cycles in the literature as comprising alternating periods of economic expansion and contraction. The criticisms of the orthodox conceptions of generic cycles suggest that the alternative conception needs to recognise that the alternating periods of expansion and contraction should be conceived of with reference to long-term trend movements in the economy. That is to say, the expansion/contraction phase is not the absolute expansion/contraction in economic activity conceived of by modern classical cycles, but rather one of relative expansion/contraction, i.e., relative to the trend. At the same time, and in contrast with most orthodox conceptions, the trend should not be seen as separate from the cyclical movements but rather as determined by these—as their average. There should therefore be an emphasis on the importance of the use of non-linear as opposed to linear trends—the use of linear trends being common in orthodox cycle identification methods, especially of growth cycles. To the extent that such non-linear trends have been conceived of in cycle analyses, they have typically been with reference to longer-term cyclical movements in the economy; so-called long cycles. In this context the present study takes the view that, while the trend matters, an elaboration of its determinants would require an unnecessary digression into a discussion of, among other things, the existence of long cycles. Rather, the point to be made here with regard to the conception of the cycle is that the cyclical movement of the economy needs to be understood as conditioned by long-run economic trends, however these might be determined, while at the same time recognising that the former has a bearing on the latter. This points to the importance of what some economists have referred to as the **path dependency** of trend movements in the economy (see, for example, Kaldor, 1934; Robinson, 1974; Setterfield, 1998).

The alternative conception of the cycle also needs to recognise that the cycle is recurrent but not periodic or symmetric. That is, cycles recur but not on the basis of any fixed periodicity or according to any particular amplitudes. The fact that cycles are recurrent suggests they need also to be seen as endogenous to the functioning of the economic system—the product of forces which are endogenous to the working of the system and not the result of random economic shocks. This is not to deny that exogenous shocks can have a bearing on cycles, since quite clearly they do. Rather, they cannot be seen as triggering *repeated* cycles, even though they can be seen as triggering major upward or downward movements in cycles at isolated moments in time. In fact, their significance for the movement of the cycle needs to be understood as depending on the juncture of the cycle at which they occur. For example, a negative exogenous shock to the system (in the form of exceptionally bad weather, for instance) would have a more muted downward influence on economic growth if it occurred in the middle of the cycle than if it occurred towards the latter stages, i.e., as the cycle matures. Similarly, a budget deficit or lower interest rates could be argued to have a bigger stimulus effect if implemented in the early stages of an economic recovery than if implemented at the end of a long period of economic expansion. In fact, the difference in timing of the implementation of such policies will most likely have very different economic consequences apart from that on economic growth, most notably with respect to inflation.

That cycles are conceived of as not periodic or symmetric means that no two cycles can be seen as being identical. This should not, however, be interpreted as the result of cycles having different root causes—different exogenous shocks; rather, it is because the actual recurrent cyclical movement of the economy is conditioned by very different factors at different points in time, including the state of the economy, economic policies, etc.

Lastly, and as implied by the preceding, cycles need to be distinguished from fluctuations and general disturbances or noise effects. Fluctuations are random, non-recurrent, alternating periods of expansion and contraction, or *vice versa*. They are the product of exogenous shocks to the system. Cycles do not preclude the phenomena of shocks, much as they do not preclude the latter having a bearing on them. Moreover, although shocks have a bearing on cycles, the cycles in turn condition the shocks. That is, fluctuations are logically of a shorter time duration than cycles, while possibly having a greater amplitude and being less symmetric than cycles. Just as the nature of shocks can vary, so can the resulting economic fluctuations generated by them. However, all things being equal, their consequences for the cyclical movement of the economy will depend on the particular cyclical juncture at which they occur. Similar magnitudes of shocks will result in larger or smaller fluctuations with corresponding upside or downside biases (i.e., a greater upward or downward movement than the preceding downward or upward movement) depending on the phase of the cycle in which they occur. As noted in Chapter 2, one consequence of the association of fluctuations with cycles in the orthodox literature is the tendency to mistake a 'double-dip' recession for two distinct cycles. Another is the tendency to mistakenly identify any downward movements in the economy with a cyclical downturn. More generally, it is to see cycles where none exist. Such misperceptions, it was noted in Chapter 2, have serious implications for policy and business decision making. Noise effects, in contrast, are inherent to most macroeconomic activity, and are manifest in most macroeconomic data series including growth rate series. They are readily differentiated from cycles, and even fluctuations, due to their relatively short periodicity and low amplitudes. They are even allowed for in standard regression analyses, by testing for the existence of non-determinate relationships.

Although general conceptualisations of cycles, particularly non-mainstream ones, also attempt to conceptualise particular phases of cycles, including so-called crisis phases, the present study does not seek to do this since, as noted above, even if one is able to unambiguously conceptualise the different phases of cycles, including their crisis phases, their identification would tend to be quite problematic. The reason for this, as the literature review makes clear, is that once it is accepted that cycles are non-regular and non-symmetric, it is unclear that particular phases of cycles can be expected to repeat in the same manner, or even repeat at all.

Figures 3.1 and 3.2 depict the various elements of the alternative conception of the cycle referred to above. Figure 3.1 shows the alternating periods of expansion and contraction phase, its movement around a trend, and its non-symmetric nature. The expansion phase begins at the point where the growth rate goes above the non-linear trend and is shown by the area to the right of the square point. The contraction phase (the shaded area) starts when the growth rate falls below the trend and is shown by the area to the right of the triangle point. The expansion phases of cycles are conceived of as being typically longer than the contraction phases, but how much longer will depend on the underlying trend. The expansion and contraction phases are shown as themselves comprising sub-phases pertaining to growth rate accelerations/decelerations and subsequent decelerations/accelerations. This means the expansion phase consists of acceleration and deceleration sub-phases. The contraction phase is similarly divided into a growth rate deceleration phase followed by an acceleration phase. The deceleration sub-phase could end with a protracted recession (or even an abrupt rupture in the system (a sudden fall in the growth rate), typically referred to as a crisis).

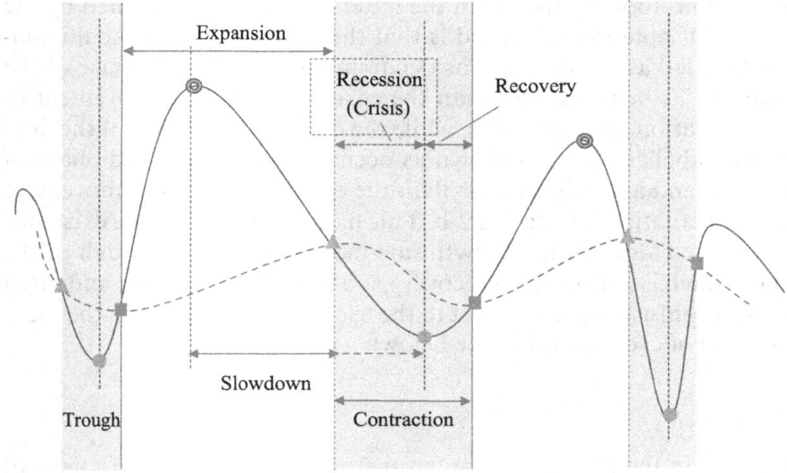

Figure 3.1 The alternative conception of generic cycles.

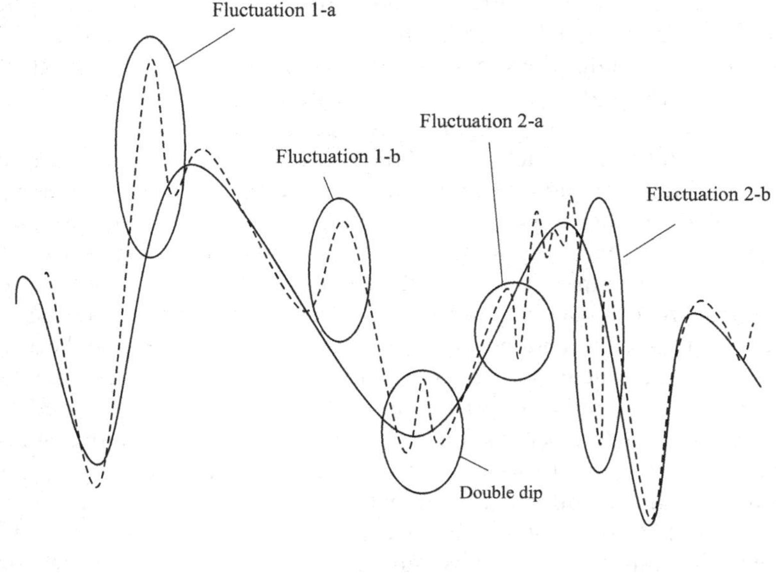

Figure 3.2 Fluctuations and cycles.

Figure 3.2 illustrates the difference between cycles (solid line) and fluctuations (dotted line), with the latter shown as conditioned by the former. Of note in this regard is that the upward part of the fluctuation labelled as 1-a is shown as occurring in the upward phase of the cycle and as being greater than the ensuing downward movement of the fluctuation labelled as 1-b, while the downward portion of the fluctuation labelled as 2-a is shown as occurring in the upward phase of the cycle and as being smaller than the ensuing downward movement of the fluctuation labelled as 2-b. This figure also depicts the existence of so-called 'double-dip' growth rate movements at the trough of the cycle, which is a short-lived recovery as a part of contraction and often leads to confusion with respect to the use of turning points in the identification of cycle bottoms (see below).

Global cycles

As noted in the preceding chapter, there are few conceptualisations of global cycles in the literature, notwithstanding the observed synchronised cyclical movement of different economies and groups of economies—hence, the need for such a conceptualisation. Given the dearth of literature on the global cycle, its conceptualisation, unlike that of the generic cycle, cannot be based on an explicit critique of corresponding mainstream conceptualisations, but should instead be informed by an extension of the above alternative conceptualisation of generic cycles.

Obviously, the point of departure for the conceptualisation of global cycles should be the synchronised and recurrent, but non-periodic and non-symmetric, expansion and contraction of economies comprising the global economic system. In a similar manner to the conceptualisation of the generic cycle, the expansion and contraction phases of the global economic cycle should be conceived of with reference to long-run trend movements in the global economy, and the source of these cycles seen as endogenous to the functioning of the global economy. Although the global economy can most certainly be accepted as comprising individual countries, and its movement even dominated by certain of these (see below), it needs to be understood as having an existence which is independent of its constituent countries; as such, it is seen as exerting an influence on all of these countries, albeit to different degrees depending on their size, structure, level of development, and integration into the global economic system. As the literature review makes clear, the growth of the global economy should be seen as dominated by the growth of the largest manufacturing economies and not the largest economies in terms of their size *per se* (see also Chapter 5). What constitutes the largest manufacturing economies in the global economy has been undergoing a considerable change in the recent past with the rise of the Japanese, South Korean, and Chinese economies, as global manufacturing powerhouses, displacing the more traditional manufacturing powerhouses—the U.S. and European economies.

As in the generic case, so too in the case of the conception of the global cycles: their conception is not intended to preclude the existence of fluctuations resulting from shocks having a bearing on the cyclical movement of the global economy, although, as with the generic case, these fluctuations need to be seen as conditioned by the movement of the cycles—the global cycles. For example, large negative shocks to large (manufacturing) economies can be expected to have only a muted negative impact on the expansion of the global economy when they occur in the upward leg of the expansion phase of the global economy, while having a considerably greater negative impact if they occur either towards the latter phases of the expansion phase or at the early stages of the contraction phase of the global economy. A case in point was the devastating Tsunami that struck Japan in 2011 and its muted consequence for the expansion of the global economy at that juncture.

Cycles pertaining to sub-global groupings of countries

The preceding section suggests that one might expect to more readily observe cycles pertaining to groupings of countries in the global economy, especially groupings of developing countries. This is because the aggregation of countries would reduce the 'noise effect' of random individual country growth rate fluctuations. The most appropriate basis for clustering of countries, i.e., those belonging to the global economic system, is arguably their level of development, economic structure, and extent and nature of integration into the global economy. One would expect more advanced, diversified, manufacturing economies to move more closely in sync with the global cycles than less advanced, raw material producers, with the latter also prone to many more fluctuations than the former. Figure 3.3 depicts the perceived relationship between the cyclical movement of the global economy and that of various groupings of economies within it.

Figure 3.4 depicts the cycles of two hypothetical sub-global groupings of countries, A and B. Although these two clusters of countries are depicted as having different cyclical movements and as being subject to a number of shocks, their cyclical movements are depicted as being conditioned in the final instance by global cycles. Thus, the troughs of the cycles in A and B are shown to roughly coincide with those of the global economy and the amplitudes of the fluctuations they experience are shown to be conditioned by the particular phases of the global cycles in which they occur.

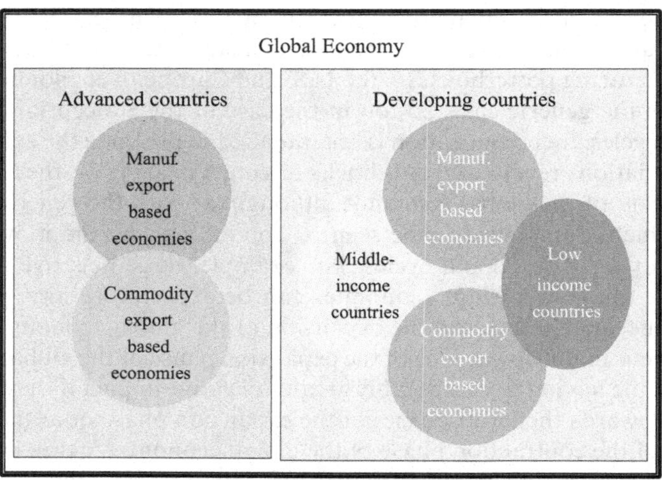

Figure 3.3 Conceptualisation of global economy.

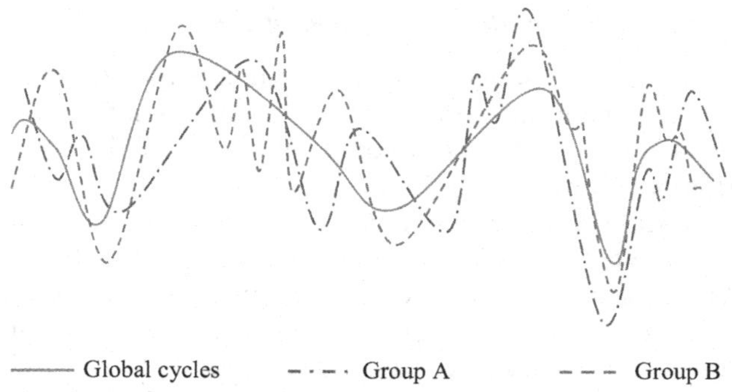

Figure 3.4 Global cycles and cycles in sub-global groupings of countries.

Alternative identification method

Generic cycles

The alternative method of cycle identification, like the alternative conceptualisation of the cycle, begins with generic cycles, and is based on the critical appraisal of the relevant mainstream literature undertaken in Chapter 2. The first implication of this critical appraisal for the alternative method of identification of cycles is, as for the mainstream literature, the importance to be attached to GDP at constant prices as depicting the state of an economy, and notwithstanding the well-known deficiencies associated with its construction, especially for poor countries with limited resources for statistical surveys (see the discussion on this point in Chapters 1 and 2). However, in contrast with much of the mainstream literature reviewed, it is the rate of change in this variable that is considered to be important for cycle identification and not its absolute value. This is because, as argued in the literature review, the real GDP growth rate is better able to capture various cycle junctures than any other macroeconomic variable and is more readily available for longer time periods than any other comparable variable for most countries. It needs to be stressed that particular importance is accorded to the non-transformed real GDP growth rate in the process of cycle identification since transformations of these data make it difficult to interpret their trend movements and use them in the construction of various required composites.

The second implication to emerge from the review of the mainstream literature on cycle identification in the preceding chapter is the importance of trends in the real GDP growth rate and the particular manner of their derivation. While much of the literature either implicitly or explicitly recognises the importance of deriving trends in the identification of cycles, the critical review of this literature argued that such trends should not be captured by any form of linear or parametric estimation method. Rather, the most appropriate method was argued to be long-run moving averages, with the time period well in excess of the duration of the average cycle and a higher weight given to more recent observations in order to provide an early indication of marked trend changes. A simple moving average is arguably one such method that meets these criteria. The major theoretical issue involved in its construction is the appropriate time period for the construction of the moving average. For the purposes of the present study this will be taken to be the average duration of the cycles, especially global cycles, over the period under consideration.[2]

The third and final implication to be derived from the critical review of the literature in the preceding chapter is that the use of cycle *maxima* and *minima* turning points for cycle identification, even in *ex post* cycle identification, is misleading. This is because the time period following cycle *maxima* and *minima,* before the cycle turns down or up, can greatly vary. Indeed, it was noted in the literature review that the use of such turning points for *ex ante* cycle identification has led to many instances of 'false' tops and bottoms being identified. That turning points cannot be used for *ex ante* identification does not, however, mean they cannot be used for *ex post* identification purposes. They can, but this should be for the purposes of identifying the duration of cycles. For this purpose, the *ex post* identification of cycle bottoms as troughs appears to be the most useful, especially since there is no intention in the present research to identify the beginnings of recessions and/or recoveries.

Global cycles

As with the conceptualisation of the global cycle, so too with its identification: the absence of any appreciable amount of mainstream (and even non-mainstream) literature on this makes it difficult to develop an alternative identification of such a cycle on the basis of a critical appraisal of the relevant literature. Instead, as with the case of the conceptualisation of the global cycle, the development of an alternative identification method for this cycle needs to be informed by an appropriate extension of the preceding alternative methodology used to identify generic cycles.

The first implication to be derived from the alternative identification of generic cycles for the identification of global cycles is that it should make use of real GDP growth rates. In this case, it should be the synchronised growth rates between countries in the form of a **non-weighted** composite of real GDP growth rates of a majority of countries comprising the world economy, i.e., simple average of the growth rates of all countries. In theory, attention should be paid to potential distortions caused by missing or manipulated data (by splicing or interpolation) in the construction of the aggregate series. In practice, however, this would make the whole exercise quite unmanageable and will not be attempted in the present study.

A second implication to be derived from the alternative identification of generic cycles for the identification of global cycles is that the latter should be done with reference to trend movements in the global economy. As with the identification of generic cycles, the trend should be constructed using moving averages and not linear estimation techniques. Also as with the identification of generic cycles, the time period for the moving average should be in excess of one cycle.

A third implication which arises from the alternative generic cycle identification for the identification of the global cycle is the *ex post* identification of this cycle on the basis of troughs. Drawing distinctions between groupings of countries, and recognising the importance of higher-income manufacturing economies for the movement of the cycle, could provide an early indication of global cycle tops and bottoms, but with the caveat noted above.

Cycles pertaining to sub-global groupings of countries

The last point made in the preceding section highlights the usefulness of identifying cycles pertaining to sub-global groupings of countries. Specifically, as noted above, the developing country groupings should be based on level of development, structure of production, and nature of integration into the global economy. The levels of development can be seen as captured by *per capita* income levels, with the usual distinctions between high-, middle-, and low-income groups providing a first approximation basis for the identification of different levels of development. The structures of the economies of developing countries that matter in capturing cyclical movements are the structures of their production and corresponding exports. In terms of their structures of production, what is important for developing countries is the extent of their dependence on primary commodity as opposed to manufacturing production. These production structures are seen as reflected in the structure of their exports, i.e., the extent of their dependence on commodity exports as opposed to manufactures. The extent and nature of integration of developing countries into the global economy is seen as similarly captured by the degree of dependence of the economy in question on exports. While it is recognised that other proxies of the extent of integration of a developing country into the global economy could be considered, such as the degree of its reliance on external savings to finance investment, it is felt this would introduce an unnecessary degree of complexity into the analysis.

As with the identification of global cycles, the starting point for the identification of cycles in sub-global groupings of countries is the construction of non-weighted real GDP composite growth rates of these groupings. The reference cycle should be taken as the global cycle, given by the movement of weighted global GDP growth rates. Divergences in trend movements in the growth rates of the unweighted clusters of developing economies in relation to trend movements in weighted global GDP growth rates could be interpreted as reflecting structural changes in the latter.

As will be argued below, the identification of cycles pertaining to the sub-global groupings of countries can further assist the important distinction to be drawn between cycles and fluctuations in particular countries, especially developing countries which are more prone to the latter. This is because such an identification would make more evident movements in real GDP growth rates of a country which correspond to cyclical movements since they can be seen as also corresponding to those of other developing counties with similar characteristics, i.e., as corresponding to the cyclical movement of the relevant cluster, notwithstanding the divergence of these cyclical movements from those pertaining to the global economy.

Notes

1 As noted in Chapter 1, those pertain to cycles in individual developing countries is not covered in this book but the key point is that they were conceived of in the manner of generic cycles but with reference to global business cycles and cycles pertaining to sub-global groupings of developing countries, allowing for the specific economic characteristics of the individual countries concerned. Reference to global cycles and cycles pertaining to clusters of developing countries in the identification of individual country cycles would aid distinctions between cycles and fluctuations. See more details, Ikeda (2018).

2 The exponential moving average provides an earlier indication of turning points when used in conjunction with data of a higher frequency (i.e., quarterly, monthly, and daily) since it attaches greater weight to more recent data. For annual data virtually no difference is observed between the exponential and simple moving average, hence the use of the latter in the present study which is based on annual data.

References

Ikeda, E. (2018, September) *Global and Developing Country Business Cycles* (Den Haag: International Institute of Social Studies, Erasmus University Rotterdam), Doctoral dissertation, Available at https://repub.eur.nl/pub/110795 [Retrieved 15 June 2019]

Kaldor, N. (1934) 'A classificatory note on the determinateness of equilibrium', *Review of Economic Studies*, 1(2), 122–36.

Robinson, J. (1974) *History versus Equilibrium* (London: Thames Polytechnic).

Setterfield, M. (1998) 'History versus equilibrium: Nicholas Kaldor on historical time and economic theory', *Cambridge Journal of Economics*, 22(5), 521–37.

4 Business cycle identification

Introduction

The aim of this chapter is to apply the alternative identification methodology developed in the preceding chapter to identify business cycles, namely global cycles and cycles pertaining to sub-global groupings of countries.[1] Emphasis is placed on the identification of cycles as opposed to fluctuations.

The alternative method for cycle identification described in Chapter 3 suggests the following. (1) The use of non-smoothed real GDP growth rates: for the identification of cycles pertaining to the global economy and sub-global groupings of countries, the alternative methodology suggests the use of non-weighted and weighted aggregates of individual country non-smoothed real GDP growth rates. (2) The use of moving averages rather than linear estimation techniques for the construction of reference trends, against which cyclical movements in real GDP are to be understood: this trend construction allows for the path dependency of the trend. (3) The use of the lowest points of the real GDP growth rates as troughs, and troughs-to-troughs for the identification of cycle periods. (4) The use of correlation analysis to capture synchronisations between sub-global groupings of countries and global cycles.

Cycle identification necessarily begins with the identification of global cycles because, as was argued above, global cycles are seen as conditioning cycles pertaining to sub-global groupings of countries. This means that the identification of cycles pertaining to sub-global groupings of developing countries should be with reference to global cycles as a benchmark. It is important to stress that this approach contrasts with the practice in most mainstream studies which attempt to identify cycles independently without reference to cycles in other countries, let alone global cycles. As indicated in Chapter 2, this is the inevitable consequence of the mainstream view of the drivers of cycles as resulting from certain random shocks.

Identifying global cycles

The aim of this section is to apply the methodology developed in the previous chapter to identify global cycles. It does so using real GDP data provided by the World Bank for 217 countries and economies for the period 1961–2017.[2] One problem with these data is that the country and related time period coverages are not uniform.[3] Real GDP data are only available for limited time periods for certain countries, especially developing countries. However, it is felt that the benefits from including those countries with missing data in the construction of growth indicators of various clusters of countries outweighs any benefits from their exclusion.

Global cycles are identified using non-smoothed composites of both non-weighted and weighted global real GDP growth rates. The former depicts the synchronised movements of the country constituents of the global economy regardless of the size of these constituents, and the latter reflect the movement of global GDP *per se*. The weights assigned to countries in the weighted composites depend on their share in world GDP on the basis of current U.S. dollars.

Figure 4.1 is a plot of two series for the period 1961–2017. The importance of using non-transformed real GDP data for the derivation of growth rates needs to be stressed. The trend is constructed using the value of the average duration of cycles between 1975 and 2017, i.e., eight years (rounded off). Taking the period of each cycle as a trough-to-trough measurement, these data show one incomplete cycle (no data on beginning of cycle), four complete cycles over this period and one unfinished cycle beginning in 2009 (no label, cycle I to IV, and cycle V in Figure 4.1, respectively). The precise dates for each cycle are given in Table 4.1.

A number of observations follow from these data. First, and most remarkably, the non-weighted and weighted series appear to move together both in terms of cycles and trends. The correlation coefficient for the two series for the time period as a whole is 0.74, indicating a high level of synchronisation (see Table 4.1). The exception is the period pertaining to cycle V (2009–17) when the correlation coefficient is appreciably lower than for the other cycles. This could be said particularly because of the ongoing structural shift in the global economy, mostly influenced by China's fall in the growth rates and their ongoing domestic structural reform (see more details, Chapter 5).

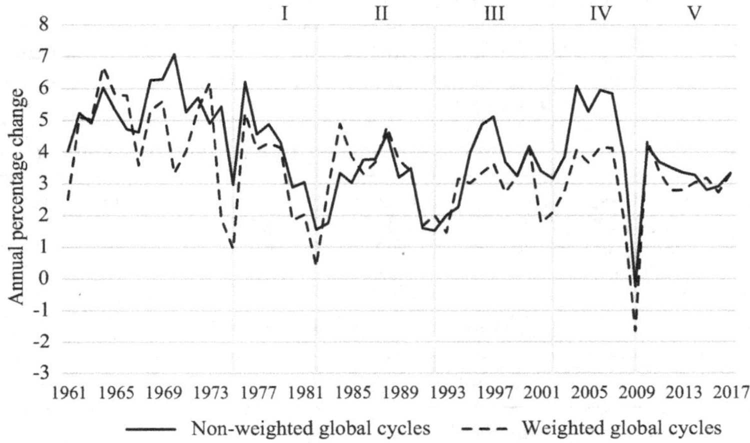

Figure 4.1 Identification of global cycles (average real growth rates), 1961–2017.
Source: World Bank World Development Indicators (WDI), author's calculation.

Notwithstanding this anomaly, the fact that the growth rates of most countries appear to move so closely together with (weighted) global GDP growth as depicted by the high correlation between the non-weighted and weighted series, suggests that there is a global gravitational force at work. This has a number of far-reaching implications, the most obvious of which is that studies of cycles in particular countries, even large advanced countries, cannot be conducted without reference to global cycles.

Second, the non-regularity of the occurrence of cycles needs to be noted. The time period for each cycle ranges from 7 to 11 years. Table 4.1 shows the time periods for each individual global cycle pertaining to both series as well as an average for all of them, including cycle V (2009–17). This provides support for the argument advanced above that cycles are non-regular and their identification (or non-identification) cannot be based on a presumed regularity of their occurrence as is the case with many orthodox identification methods. In addition, this finding proves that Juglar cycles exists at the global level.

Third, the amplitudes of each cycle differ. The amplitudes are taken to be the highest deviation from peak (*maxima*) to trend added to the highest deviation of the following trough (*minima*) to trend, following the existing standard calculation reviewed in Chapter 2. Table 4.1 shows that the amplitudes of all five cycles are different, ranging from

Table 4.1 Global cycle identification: dates, duration, amplitude, and synchronisation, 1975–2017

Cycle No.	*Non-weighted global cycles*				*Synchronisation*
	Date	*Duration*[a]	*Amplitudes*		
			Expansion	*Contraction*	*Correlation*[d]
I	1975–1982	7	0.73	2.25	0.99
II	1982–1992	10	1.48	1.89	0.84
III	1992–2002	10	2.02	0.99	0.45
IV	2002–2009	7	1.98	4.46	1.00
V[b]	2009–(2017)	(8)	(0.02)	(0.64)	(0.26)
Avg.[b,c]		8.5 (8.4)	1.55 (1.24)	2.4 (2.05)	0.71 (0.82)

Cycle No.	*Weighted global cycles*			
	Date	*Duration*[a]	*Amplitude*	
			Expansion	*Contraction*
I	1975–1982	7	1.29	3.64
II	1982–1993	11	1.25	3.82
III	1993–2001	8	0.76	2.50
IV	2001–2009	8	1.78	5.28
V[b]	2009–(2017)	(8)	(0.49)	(1.50)
Avg.[b,c]		8.5 (8.4)	1.27 (1.11)	3.81 (3.35)

a Duration is in years (this also applies to Tables 4.2 and 4.3).
b Values in the brackets are for the unfinished cycle V. Period averages include data pertaining to this cycle (this also applies to values provided in Tables 4.2 and 4.3).
c Avg. is Average (this also applies to values provided in Tables 4.2 and 4.3).
d Correlation between non-weighted and weighted global cycles.

around 0.6% to 6.5% (sum of expansion and contraction). The largest amplitude among the five pertains to that of cycle IV (2002–9), mainly because of the unusually sharp and considerable fall in economic growth during the 2007–9 crisis. In addition, the amplitudes of the contraction phases are generally greater than those of the expansion phases. This reinforces the point made in Chapters 2 and 3, that amplitudes vary and are asymmetric, making it misleading to base cycle identification on presumed similar amplitudes as some cycle identification methods do. It is also of note that the amplitudes of the two series are on average roughly the same (see Table 4.1).

Fourth, the additional analysis on the deviation from the trend on the average real growth rates shows that the time duration from the cycle peak to the fall of the growth rate below trend, i.e., the movement of the economy into its contraction phase, varies quite considerably between cycles, making the use of cycle *maxima* as 'turning points' of dubious value. Although similar divergences between cycle *minima* and transitions to the expansion phases of cycles are observed across the four cycles, they are not as marked as the divergences between cycle *maxima* and transitions to the contraction phases of the cycles. What is startling is that from 2011 onwards the non-weighted series has been showing the cycle to be continuously in a contraction phase (i.e., deviation is below zero), while the weighted series suggests such a contraction ended in 2013 (i.e., deviation is above zero).

Fifth, the trend movements of the two global real GDP composites diverge from the beginning of the 1990s, providing two contrasting views of movements in the global economy. The fact that the non-weighted series is continuously above the weighted series would confirm the perception that less developed, smaller economies tend to experience relatively higher growth rates than the larger, more developed economies (that are given the larger weights in the weighted series). The divergence of the trend is clearly evident since the beginning of the 1990s, when the non-weighted series started to show higher trend movements.

One last point to be made in the context of the identification of the global cycle is the importance to be accorded to the non-linear estimation of the trend. To begin with, the shape of the linear trend by definition depends on the starting date of the data. Thus, while the trend depicted by taking a starting date of 1968 is clearly downward, the trend depicted by taking the starting date as 1992, for example, is upward. Moreover, and following from this point, taking linear trends means it is often not possible to distinguish between sub-periods of relative strength and weakness. While the linear trend shows the entire period from 1961 to 2017 to be one of continuous economic weakness as it shows the straight downward line, a non-linear trend constructed starting with 1968 suggests that, although the period as a whole is one of weakening economic growth (the peak of the second trend cycle being lower than the peak of the first), one can discern sub-periods of relative economic strength such as 1986–90, 1995–98, and 2004–7 (see Figure 4.2). In fact, one of the consequences of using a linear trend in the identification of cycles, and in this case global cycles,[4] is that it gives a distorted picture of expansions and contractions—which are conceived of in relation to the trend. For example, considering the movement of global real GDP growth in relation to the linear trend suggests that the period from 2010 to 2014 can be characterised as one of (relative) expansion in the global

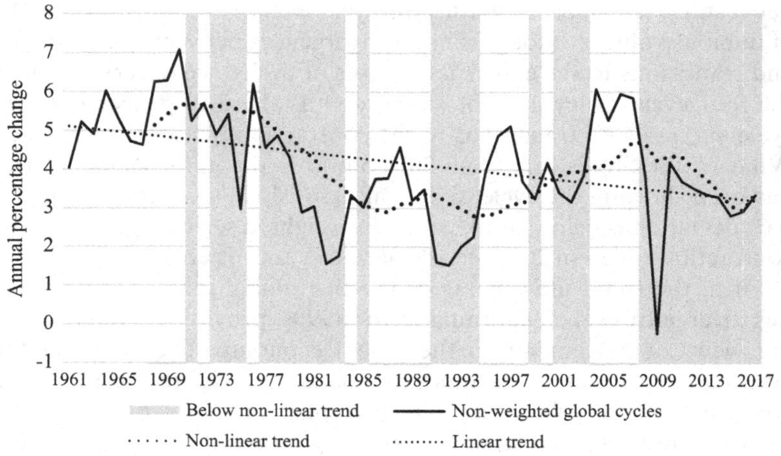

Figure 4.2 Relative expansion and contraction phases in global cycles (average real growth rates), 1961–2017.

Source: World Bank World Development Indicators (WDI), author's calculation.

economy as the former is above the latter, while the movement of global real GDP in relation to the non-linear trend shows this period to be one of continuous weakness (see Figure 4.2)—a view shared by most observers of the global economy, including the central bankers of the dominant global economies who considered it to be a period of such pronounced weakness that it required extraordinary monetary and fiscal policies to compensate.

Cycles pertaining to sub-global groupings of countries

This section attempts to identify the characteristics of cycles pertaining to sub-global clusters of developing countries, grouped according to their levels of development and economic structures.[5] As in the global economy case in the section above, the data used for the identification of these cycles are aggregated and non-transformed real growth rates. The identification of cycles pertaining to such clusters is based on a comparison of a non-weighted composite of the growth rates of the countries comprising the cluster and the **weighted** global cycles, i.e., global benchmark cycles. The aim is to see the extent to which the cycles of countries comprising various sub-groupings move with global cycles, where the latter are depicted by the weighted average of countries comprising the global economy.

The period for the identification of such cycles is 1983 to 2017, depending on the availability of the data on which the classifications are based.[6] The period covers three complete and one unfinished cycles (i.e., cycles II to V shown in Figure 4.1). The basis for the different country clusters is explained in the sections below.[7] Country compositions of different groupings vary from cycle to cycle depending on changes in the level of development and the economic structure of the individual countries within each cluster. Modifications of country clusters are made in accordance with the criteria adopted at the beginning (first year) of each reference cycle, i.e., 1983, 1994, 2002, and 2010. Since data pertaining to clusters of countries based on the level of development are only available from 1987, the data pertaining to these clusters of countries for the first cycle (i.e., cycle II) are based on backward extrapolations. Reconstituting country groupings between cycles is considered necessary in order to reflect changes in the structures of individual countries over time, and indispensable if misperceptions are to be avoided. It also reinforces the points made about the problems with conventional identification techniques which are by their nature unable to take into account such changes. The non-linear trend of cluster cycles is derived in the same manner as that in the weighted global series. Although the average duration of cycles is expected to vary across the groupings of economies, to facilitate their comparison with one another and with the global cycles, the same numbers of years are used for the construction of the moving average, i.e., eight years. Data limitations mean that the trends for various clusters are only available from 1990. Therefore, the amplitudes of cycle II are only based on the data between 1990 and 1994. This is, admittedly, a serious limitation of the approach.

Level of development

The classification of countries according to their level of development follows the widely used Gross National Income (GNI) per capita classification made by the World Bank. To be specific, on the basis of GNI per capita the World Bank classifies countries as high-, upper middle-, lower middle-, or low-income countries,[8] with the first seen as representing the advanced countries and the latter three typically seen as constituting the developing countries. The sub-global groupings of countries to be identified in this section are at the most aggregated level, and these are advanced and developing countries.[9] The numbers of countries included and the detailed country constituents in each cycle identification are noted in Appendix Table A.1. To identify cycles in advanced and developing countries, countries in the two groupings are clustered on a non-weighted basis and the cycles pertaining to the cyclical movement in growth rates of these two groupings are then compared to the global weighted cycle as the reference cycle, i.e., benchmark cycle. Figure 4.3 depicts composite weighted global economy growth rates (as derived above) alongside aggregated non-weighted economic growth rates for both advanced and developing countries over the period 1983–2017. What is observed from these figures is the following.

First, the cyclical growth rate movements of the advanced and developing countries are synchronised with those of the global economy. The correlation coefficients for the synchronisation of the growth rates of these clusters of economies with those of the global economy are roughly 0.8 and 0.5, respectively, for the period as a whole (see Table 4.2). One important point of note is the apparent decline in synchronisation of the cyclical movement of growth in the developing countries with that of the weighted global cycle (and advanced economies in particular) since 2011 (see Figure 4.3). The correlation between 2011 and 2017 for these two series is minus 0.08, while that of whole period V is 0.43. This point will be returned to in the discussion

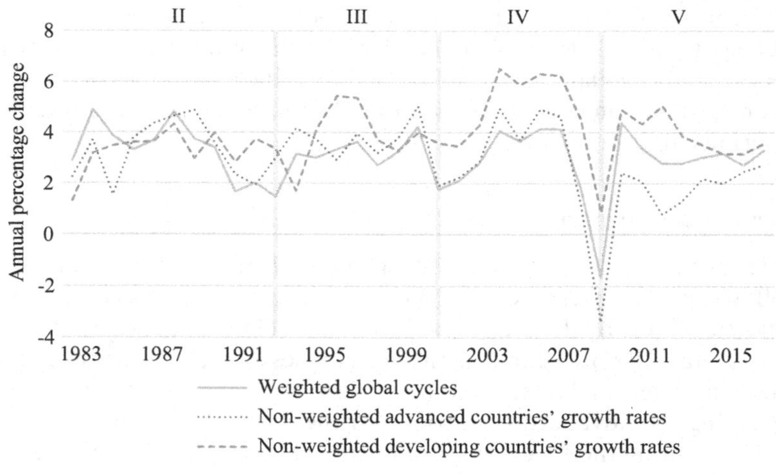

Figure 4.3 Identification of cycles in advanced and developing countries, 1983–2017.

Source: World Bank WDI, author's calculation.

ble 4.2 Identification and nature of cycles in advanced and developing countries, 1983–2017

ef. cle[a]	*Advanced countries*				*Developing countries*			
	Troughs	*Duration*	*Amplitudes*[b]	*Correlation*[c]	*Troughs*	*Duration*	*Amplitudes*[b]	*Correlation*[c]
	1992	10	1.38	0.54	1994[d]	11	1.72	0.26
	2001	9	3.16	0.89	1999	5	3.18	0.25
	2009	8	7.91	1.00	2009	10	5.25	0.97
	(2017)	(8)	(2.16)	(0.45)	(2017)	(8)	(2.59)	(0.43)
vg.		9 (8.75)	4.15 (3.65)	0.81 (0.72)		8.67 (8.5)	3.38 (3.18)	0.5 (0.48)

The time period for each cycle corresponds to those of the weighted global cycles (i.e., reference cycle) in Table 4.1 (this also applies to Table 4.3).
Amplitude is calculated with reference to the global cycles (this also applies to Table 4.3).
The correlation is with respect to the weighted global cycles (this also applies to Table 4.3).
The trough of the previous cycle for developing countries is 1983.

of the country drivers of global cycles in Chapter 5 since it has certain obvious implications for the explanation of these drivers.

Second, the troughs of the cycles in the advanced and developing countries are roughly the same as those of the weighted global cycles, although troughs in the cycles of the developing countries can be seen to lead or lag those of the advanced countries until cycle V (2009–17). The average duration of cycles in the advanced and developing countries is roughly the same but the latter is slightly shorter than the global cycles (i.e., 8.75, 8.5, and 8.75 years, respectively, between cycle II and V), regardless of these differences in the observed troughs. As with the global cycles, the duration for both clusters of countries, i.e., advanced and developing countries, varies between cycles, contrary to the assumptions underlying many of the mainstream methods used in cycle identification (as discussed in Chapter 2).

Third, and also contrary to the assumption of many orthodox cycle identification methods, cycle amplitudes can be seen to vary between cycles. This is evident for the global cycles as well as cycles pertaining to clusters of advanced and developing countries (see Table 4.2). Curiously, cycle amplitudes for advanced countries appear to be greater than for developing countries.[10]

Structure of the economy

This section aims to identify cycles for groupings of developing countries based on perceived differing structures of these economies. Since the focus is on developing countries, the key distinction is between manufacturing and primary goods-based (i.e., commodity-based) export economies. Primary goods exporters comprise exporters of food, of fuel, of ores and metals, and of agricultural raw materials.[11] Classification of countries into various groupings is on the basis of export composition, with this composition seen as reflecting the production structures of the economies. A point to note in this context is that, although food and fuel production are usually regarded as part of manufacturing production in general GDP computations, for the purposes of the present study, a distinction will be made between the three, and food and fuels are included in the primary goods. The reason for this distinction is that the extent to which economies specialise in and export one or another of these three appears to be important in explaining different cyclical movements.

Composites of countries based on types of exports are developed in accordance with the World Bank classifications of export products discussed above. The countries are classified as specialising in the export of one product category or another according to the preponderance of the value of the product in the total value of their exports.[12] The product groupings which are used in the following analysis are manufactures and primary-commodities. As with the identification of country groupings of cycles based on levels of development, in their identification with respect to economic structures, the reference cycle will be taken as the aggregate weighted global cycle; for cycles pertaining to groupings of countries the basis for the identification of cycles will be taken to be the non-weighted aggregation of non-smoothed real GDP growth rates of the constituent countries over the period 1983–2017. The classifications based on the above-mentioned economic structures are taken as changing with each cycle, depending on perceived shifts in the structure of exports of the countries concerned. The numbers of countries in each classification and details of the countries included in each classification provided in Appendix Table A.1. It shows that over the period under consideration increasing numbers of economies have shifted from primary products exports to manufacturing exports, especially from 1983 onwards. The identified cycles pertaining to groupings of manufacturers and commodity producers are presented in Figure 4.4. The first thing to note is that the troughs of primary commodity-based economies only coincide with those of the global cycles in cycle IV (2001–9), while those of manufacturing-based economies correspond with the global cycles in cycle II (1983–93) as well. Second, it is apparent that the cyclical movements of the clusters of developing countries are increasingly synchronised with those of the global cycles over the period 1983–2017, with the correlation of the manufacturing-based developing economies being higher than that of

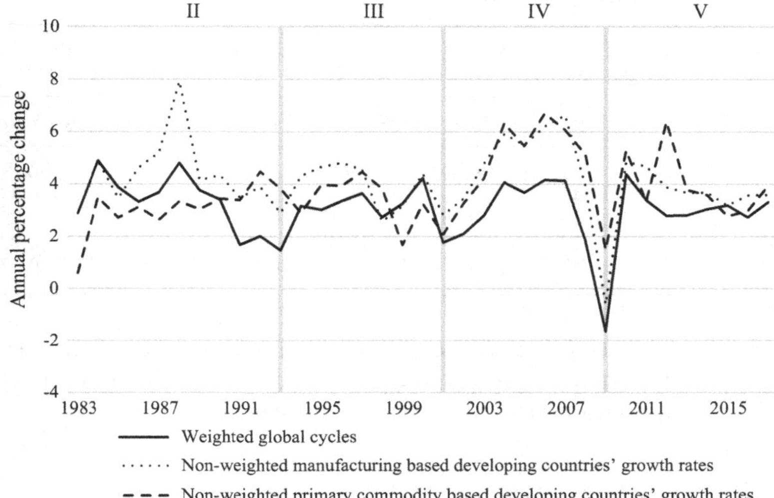

Figure 4.4 Identification of cycles in manufacturing- and commodity-export based developing countries, 1983–2017.

Source: World Bank World Development Indicators (WDI), author's calculation.

the primary commodity-based economies (with coefficients of around 0.8 and 0.3, respectively). At the same time, it is also evident that the extent of the synchronisation for both clusters varies between cycles (see Table 4.3). In that light, it could be argued that the recent (post-2009) apparent decline in synchronisation of cycles pertaining to both clusters of developing countries with the global cycle (see Table 4.3) could indicate the beginning of a de-coupling of these economies from the global economy. However, it could also be argued that the apparent fall in the degree of synchronisation since 2009 is simply the product of the usual periodic shifts in global production and trade, which take place over time and in the context of the long-term increase in economic integration between countries (see next chapter for an elaboration of this point). It is noteworthy in this context that the trend growth rates for both manufacturing- and primary commodity-based economies have tended to move with those of the global economy, while being appreciably above the latter for the period as a whole. Third, in keeping with all the other cycles identified above, the duration of the cycles for manufacturing and commodity exporters varies between cycles (see Table 4.3). Fourth, the overall average amplitudes

Table 4.3 Identification and nature of cycles in manufacturing- and primary commodity-based developing countries, 1983–2017

Ref. cycle	*Manufacturing-based developing countries*				*Primary commodity-based developing countries*			
	Troughs	*Duration*	*Amplitudes*	*Correlation*	*Troughs*	*Duration*	*Amplitudes*	*Correlati*
II	1993	9	0.78	0.69	1994	10	1.55	−0.18
III	1998	5	2.40	0.65	1999	5	2.90	0.38
IV	2009	11	6.49	0.99	2009	10	4.59	0.92
V	(2017)	(8)	(2.29)	(0.71)	(2017)	(8)	(3.83)	(0.23)
Avg.		8.33 (8.25)	3.22 (2.99)	0.78 (0.76)		8.33 (8.25)	3.01 (3.22)	0.37 (0.

of the cycles pertaining to the manufacturing-based economies are higher than those pertaining to the primary commodity-based economies, with amplitudes for both varying between cycles.

Notes

1 As mentioned in Chapter 1, the identification of the cycles in the sub-divided clusters within sub-global groupings of developing countries and individual countries is out of scope in this book, yet the findings in this chapter are relevant to these cycles. This is because these cycles need to be identified with reference to the global cycles, with the degree being dependent on the particular economic structure of the country (and its evolution over the time period under consideration) (see more details, Ikeda, 2018).
2 These and all other data used in this chapter were accessed on 21 March, 2019.
3 The numbers of countries and economies that data are available steadily increased from less than 100 at the beginning of 1960s to around 200 by the late 1990s.
4 This also applies to the weighted series.
5 It is recognised that other criteria have been used to cluster economies, including degree of openness and geographic location. However, it is felt that the criteria used in the present study are adequate given its purpose—to show how developing countries with similar economic structures tend to follow similar cyclical patterns with respect to global cycles.
6 Due to the construction of the aggregated series, for the cycle of II will not include the year of 1982.
7 Differences in the numbers of countries included in the various clusters should not alter the results of the analysis as well. This is because all countries can be expected to move in more or less the same way given that they are part of the same global system (see Chapter 3) and the purpose of the construct is to develop an indicator of the synchronised growth movement of the clusters as a whole.
8 For the historical threshold and country classification on the basis of their per capita by World Bank, see World Bank's 'Historical classification by income in XLS format' (https://datahelpdesk.worldbank.org/knowledgebase/articles/906519).

9 For further identification of cycles in sub-divided clusters of middle- and low-income countries, see Ikeda (2018). The key finding is that the middle-income countries tend to have a higher degree of synchronisation with the global economy than lower-income countries.

10 One explanation could be the relatively weaker growth performance of the advanced countries over this period and the corresponding larger magnitudes of falls in their growth rates during cyclical downturns.

11 For the identification of cycles in the exporters of food, fuel, and ores and metals, see Ikeda (2018). It has shown that the synchronisation of cycles in growth rates of all different categories of developing countries with the global economy tend to be generally the same, while there are differences in observed nature of cycles.

12 The relative preponderance of a particular type of export is given by calculating its percentage share in total merchandise exports (as given by the data from the World Bank's WDI).

Reference

Ikeda, E. (2018, September) *Global and Developing Country Business Cycles* (Den Haag: International Institute of Social Studies, Erasmus University Rotterdam), Doctoral dissertation, Available at https://repub.eur.nl/pub/110795 [Retrieved 15 June 2019].

Databases

World Bank Country and Lending Groups. https://datahelpdesk.worldbank.org/knowledgebase/articles/906519

World Development Indicators (WDI). http://databank.worldbank.org/data/reports.aspx?source=world-development-indicators

5 Drivers of business cycles

Introduction

The aim of this chapter is to investigate the drivers of cycles in the global economy, and for sub-global groupings of developing countries.[1] The particular focus of the drivers of global cycles is what might be referred to as their country drivers—those countries which exert the greatest influence on the movement of the global economy.[2] From the literature review in Chapter 2, it should be apparent that the concern here is to establish whether the countries which drive the global economy are the large economies *per se,* or, more specifically, the large manufacturing economies. For the sub-global groupings of developing countries, the aim is to investigate whether cycles in their economic growth rates are driven by cycles in global economic growth rates. To be precise, the aim is to establish whether cycles in the global economy are the main drivers of cycles in these economies. This relates to the discussion in the literature as to whether cycles in developing country economies can be considered to be mostly internally or externally driven, with the former being identified with random domestic shocks and the latter with the movement of the global economy, i.e., global cycles.

The chapter is divided into two parts corresponding to the above-mentioned objectives. The first part considers the country drivers of the global cycles; the second part analyses the drivers of cycles pertaining to sub-global groupings of developing countries, paying particular attention to the trade channel with the importance of cyclical movements in the global economy as the major drivers of such cycles.

The growth rates of sub-global groupings of developing countries are taken to be the weighted averages of countries comprising the clusters. The growth rates are based on non-smoothed real GDP data provided by the World Bank. The real export growth data is derived by subtracting the change in trade-weighted dollar index by the U.S.

Federal Reserve Board (FED) from the growth in merchandise export by World Bank. The groupings of countries are composited in the same manner as in the previous chapter.

The empirical methods used to investigate the drivers of cycles in this chapter will comprise exploratory data and econometric analyses. Most weight will be given to the former for reasons given in Chapter 1, but some weight will also be accorded to the results obtained by means of latter to support the exploratory data findings. The results and discussion of the econometric analyses are presented in detail in the Appendix in this chapter. These results will be referred to in the main text where it is deemed appropriate.

Country drivers of global cycles

This section addresses the issue of the country drivers of global cycles. The global cycles to be explained are those depicted by growth rates of weighted global GDP at constant prices.

It was argued in Chapters 2 and 3 that a crucial element missing from standard accounts of the drivers of cycles in general, and global cycles in particular, is the importance that should be accorded to manufacturing production (and exports of manufactured products). Figure 5.1 is a plot of the annual growth rates of global GDP at constant prices and real manufacturing production growth between 1997

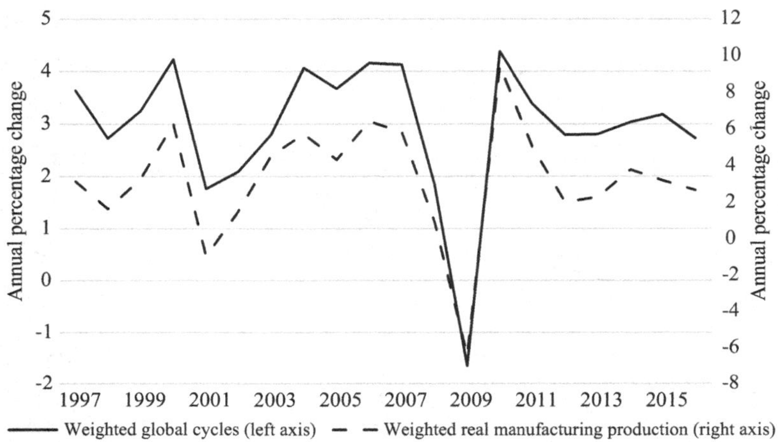

Figure 5.1 Weighted global real GDP and manufacturing production growth, 1997–2016.

Source: World Bank World Development Indicators (WDI), author's calculation.

and 2016.[3] These data appear to confirm the hypothesised importance ascribed to manufacturing as the most important driver of real GDP growth.[4] Further support of this observed relationship is provided by the results of bivariate Ordinary Least Squares (OLS) regression (see Appendix section on global cycles and global manufacturing production). The important point to note about the regression results is the value of the parameter estimate for the manufacturing variable. This suggests that the contribution of global manufacturing growth is greater than what would be suggested by the proportion of global GDP that it accounts for.

What the preceding suggests is that the major driver of the global economy and global cycles in particular is not the growth of, or cycles in, the largest economies *per se* but rather the growth of, and cycles in, the largest manufacturing producers. Figure 5.2 provides data on who these producers are. Specifically, it depicts the global manufacturing share of the large manufacturing economies, including Asian countries (excluding China and Japan)[5] who have been showing the increasing presence in the global manufacturing production. It shows that, until recently, the largest manufacturers—i.e., the United States, European Union (Germany, France, and Italy), the United Kingdom, and Japan—have also been the largest economies in terms of GDP size. Indeed, up to around 2009/10, the largest manufacturer was also the largest economy in the world; the U.S. economy. However, from

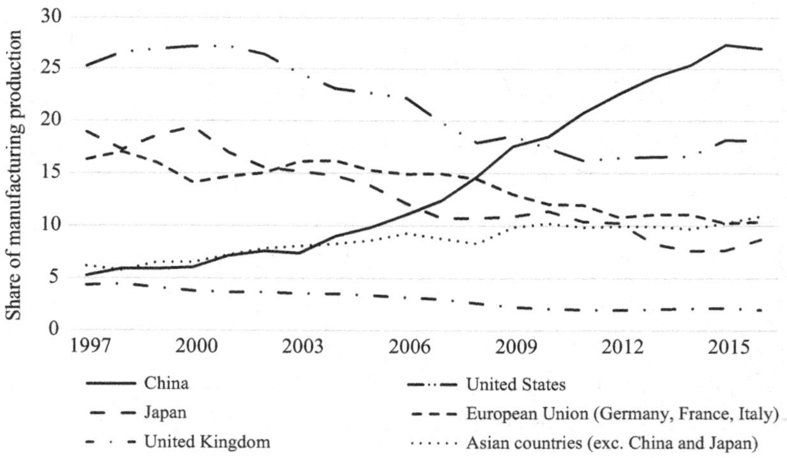

Figure 5.2 Shares of global manufacturing production (value added), 1997–2016. Source: World Bank WDI, author's calculation.

this date onwards, China surpassed the United States as the largest manufacturing economy, notwithstanding the fact that its economy is still smaller than that of the United States in terms of absolute GDP (in current U.S. dollars).[6] What Figure 5.2, in conjunction with Figure 5.1, suggests is that, contrary to assumptions made in many studies of the drivers of the global economy, it is no longer the United States but China that appears to be at the helm of the global economy. It is China, as the largest manufacturer, that is currently the main driver of global economic cycles. Indeed, the divergence of the cycles of nearly all developing countries and many advanced countries from that of the U.S. economy over the course of the most recent global cycle could well be indicative of precisely this shift in the global economic dynamic.

Although it could be too early to definitively conclude that China has assumed the role of the principal driver of the global economy, further evidence that this may well be the case at the present juncture comes in the form of correlation coefficients for the co-movement of global cycles and growth rate cycles of selected individual large (manufacturing) economies. The data is presented in Figure 5.3, with the former is the non-weighted global GDP growth rate series. What this figure suggests is that, while the advanced countries, particularly those responsible for most manufactured exports, could be said to have been

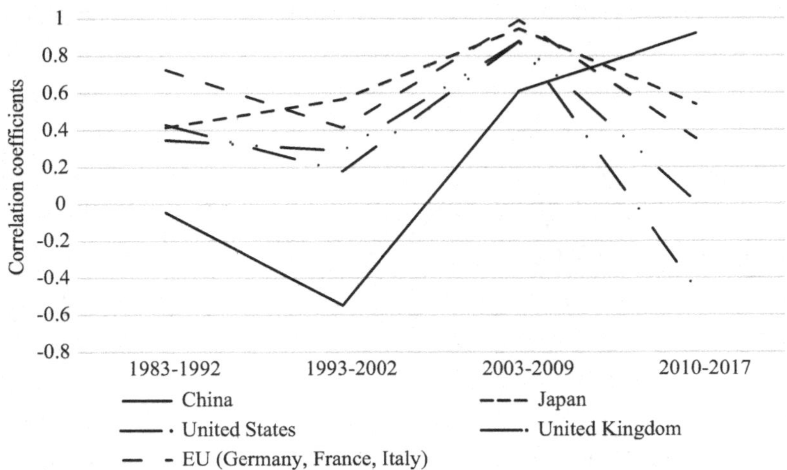

Figure 5.3 Correlation of selected economies' real growth rates with non-weighted global cycles, 1983–2017.

Note: EU (Germany, France, Italy) is weighted.

Source: World Bank World Development Indicators (WDI), author's calculation.

the major drivers of the global economy up to cycle IV (i.e., until 2009), from the commencement of the present cycle, this role appears to have shifted to China.[7] Interestingly, and reinforcing the point made above, in the most recent cycle, the degrees of correlation between the dominant global manufacturers and the global cycles appear to have changed compared to the recent past. Specifically, the data appear to show that the correlation between the growth of China's real GDP and global GDP is rising while those between all other large manufacturers and the global economy is falling. Indeed, it is this shift that perhaps explains the observed divergence from 2009 onwards of both weighted and non-weighted global GDP growth rates from the growth rates of many clusters of developing countries shown in the previous chapter (see Figure 4.1 in the previous chapter).

More evidence of China as the major country driver of global cycles, particularly since 2009, comes in the form of the recent massive fiscal and credit expansion undertaken by the Chinese authorities to revive their flagging economy, which translated into a major boost to all other major economies.[8] Monthly leading indicators data provided by the OECD[9] (see Figure 5.4) appear to show that this stimulus resuscitated not only the Chinese economy, but also the global economy as a whole. Of particular note in Figure 5.4 is the prior movement of the leading indicators of the Chinese economy as compared with those for the G7 group of countries as a whole, not only with respect to

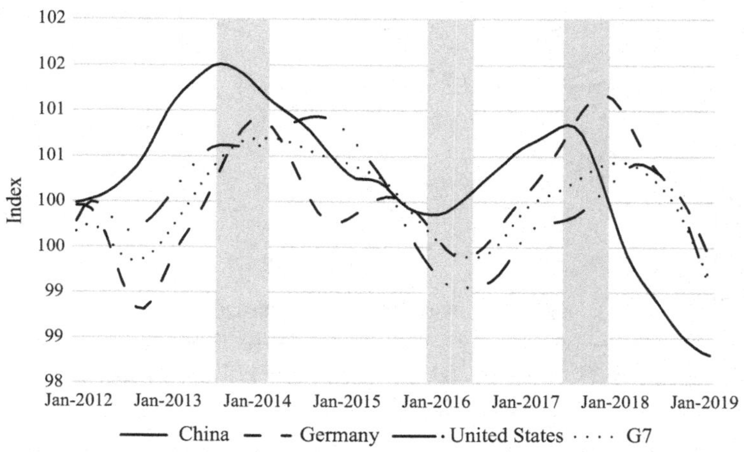

Figure 5.4 Leading composite indicators for China, the United States, Germany, and the G7 countries, Jan 2012–Mar 2019.

Source: OECD. Chart by author.

their recovery but also the preceding downward movement (see shaded areas).[10,11] The point that needs reiterating in this context is that, like all economies comprising the global economic system, China too is impacted by the movement of the global economy, notwithstanding the fact that it may now be considered to be one of the major drivers of the latter, if not its principal driver.

Drivers of cycles in sub-global groupings of countries

This section investigates the drivers of cycles in the sub-global groupings of developing countries. As with the identification of cycles in the previous chapter, particular attention is paid to the level of development and the structure of the economy in the construction of the clusters. Following from the literature review, and in particular the growth theory advanced by Kaldor, as well as the earlier analysis in the present chapter, the aim is to show the importance of merchandise exports in driving economic growth and, therefore, cycles in these clusters of developing countries. The country composition of each of the clusters is given in Appendix Table A.1. The compositions of these clusters are modified at the troughs of each of the global cycles to reflect the changing structures of the individual developing countries, in the same manner as the identification of cycles in the previous chapter.

Level of development

The first sub-grouping of developing countries that requires consideration is that based on the level of development, one comprising developing countries as a whole, which consists of upper middle-, lower middle-, and low-income countries.[12,13] As in Chapter 4, the levels of development are depicted by per capita GNI (see the country composition in Appendix Table A.1).

Figure 5.5 is a plot of the growth rates of weighted real GDP and weighted real total merchandise exports for developing countries over the period 1983 to 2017 (i.e., cycles II to V of the weighted global reference cycles). What the figure shows is that, in general, the two series move together, and that when they do not, exports lead economic growth. The correlation coefficient for the co-movement of the two series over the whole period is 0.69, with higher correlation coefficients for the co-movement of the two series in cycle IV (2001–9). The implied positive impact of the export growth of developing countries on their economic growth is further supported by OLS (see Appendix section on merchandise export growth of developing countries as a whole and

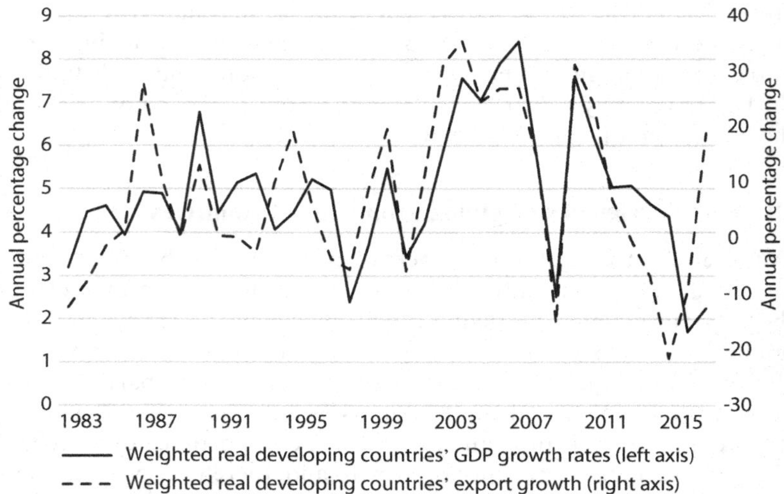

Figure 5.5 Weighted real merchandise export and real GDP growth rates of developing countries, 1983–2017.

Source: World Bank WDI, FED, author's calculation.

their real GDP growth). It may be seen from these results that the OLS parameter estimates are of the expected magnitudes given the mean values of the two variables.

Structure of the economy

The second sub-grouping of developing countries to be considered is those based on the structure of the economy. As in Chapter 4, the clusters considered most appropriate are with respect to the major type of export: manufacturing and primary goods-based (i.e., commodity-based) export economies (see Appendix Table A.1 for the country compositions of each groups).[14]

Figure 5.6 presents a plot of growth rates of weighted real GDP and manufacturing exports in constant U.S. dollars for a group of manufacturing export economies. The figure shows a fair degree of synchronisation between the two series; where this is not the case, export earnings growth leads economic growth. As can be seen from the figure, such lead-lag relationships are evident in 1987–88, 1992–98, and 2015–16. Correlation coefficients for the co-movement of the two variables (i.e., 0.69), reinforces the impression of the close synchronisation

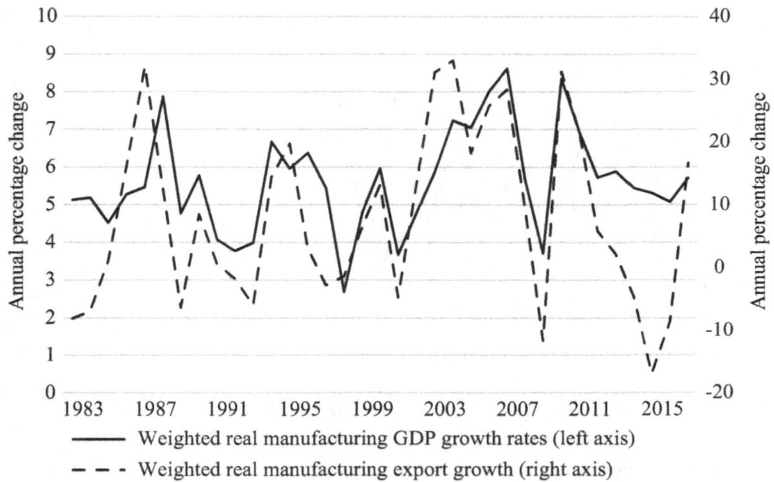

Figure 5.6 Weighted real manufacturing export and real growth rates of manufacturing-based developing countries, 1983–2017.

Source: World Bank WDI, FED, author's calculation.

of their movement, especially since the cycle VI (2001–9). The high degree of co-movement of the two variables should also not be surprising, given the increasing considerable weight of China in this cluster (i.e., up to around 50% of the total, especially in cycle V) and the well-known export basis of its manufacturing-led economic growth process (see also Hausmann et al., 2007; Rodrik, 2007).

OLS regression results presented in the Appendix section also support the contention that the real GDP growth of the manufacturing-based cluster of economies is considerably influenced by its export growth, although it should perhaps be noted that the estimated parameter value for the dependent variable (0.068) is lower than that for the regression of total merchandise export growth on total real GDP growth for all developing countries (0.074) (see equations A.4 and A.3 in Appendix). In terms of economic significance, this suggests that the growth rates of manufacturing exporters is likely to be less sensitive to export earnings than in the case of commodity exporters. The introduction of lags into the regression analysis did not have any appreciable consequences for the results (see equation A.6, Appendix).[15]

Figure 5.7 is a plot of the growth rates of weighted real GDP and primary commodity exports in constant U.S. dollars for a cluster of primary

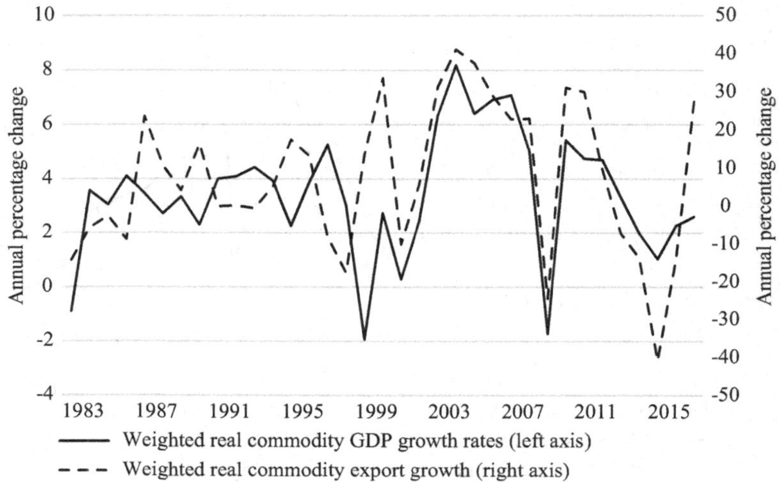

Figure 5.7 Weighted real primary commodity export and real growth rates of primary commodity-based developing countries, 1983–2017.

Source: World Bank WDI, FED, author's calculation.

commodity-exporting developing countries. The figure shows that up to the early 2000s the degree of synchronisation between the two data series is quite low but rises appreciably from this date onwards. Confirmation of this is given by the correlation coefficients for the various cycles covering the period as a whole. For cycles prior to 2000, the correlation coefficients are quite low (minus 0.12) but rise thereafter (0.8 between 2000 and 2017). The increased synchronisation of the two variables suggests primary commodity-based economies became more enmeshed in the global economic system and more dependent on their export earnings.

OLS regression results also provide support for the hypothesised relationship between export earnings and economic growth for the commodity-producing developing countries. The parameter value for the estimated relationship in the commodity-producing developing countries is, as expected, higher than in the case of manufactures: 0.069 as compared with 0.068 (see equations A.4 and A.7 in Appendix). The higher expected parameter value is because the parameter value for the corresponding relationship for all developing countries was shown to be greater than for manufacturing developing countries above. These results support those found in the literature pointing to growth rates of exporters of primary commodities being more sensitive to export earnings than those of exporters of manufactures due, on the one hand, to their greater dependence on the export earnings and, on the other hand, to the greater volatility in the prices of these products.[16]

Appendix to the chapter

Econometric analysis of the drivers of business cycles

This Appendix presents the results of econometric analyses with a view to supporting (or otherwise) the exploratory data findings of Chapter 5 with regard to the drivers of business cycles. Although the weaknesses of the use of such empirical methods in business cycle analyses were noted in Chapters 1–3, it is felt that, when used in conjunction with the exploratory data analysis of Chapter 5, they could serve to strengthen the findings of that chapter.

The structure of the presentation of the results of the econometric analysis in this Appendix largely follows the structure of the exploratory data analysis in Chapter 5. Specifically, it will be organized into three sections: the first looks at econometric evidence pertaining to the relationship between cycles in economic and manufacturing production growth in the global economy, the second looks at the econometric evidence pertaining to the relationship between cycles in economic and export growth of all developing countries (i.e., level of development) and the third the econometric evidence pertaining to the relationship between cycles in economic and export growth of clusters of developing countries (i.e., structure of the economy). The relevant model specifications, data, results and their interpretation will be elaborated on in each section below. The software used to derive the econometric estimation results is STATA SE version 12.

Global cycles and global manufacturing production

The analysis in Chapter 5 found that the growth of global manufacturing production drives global GDP growth (see Figure 5.1). This relationship is tested using time series regression methods and data for the period 1997 to 2016. The data of concern for this analysis are the same as those presented in Figure 5.1, i.e., weighted non-smoothed real global manufacturing production growth rates and weighted global real GDP growth rates over the time period 1997–2016. The descriptive statistics for the two variables presented in Table A.5.1 show that the movement of the manufacturing variable is greater than that of

Table A.5.1 Descriptive statistics for selected variables

	Mean	*SD*	*Min*	*Max*	*No. of obs.*
Real global growth rates	2.97	1.30	−1.65	4.38	21
Real global manufacturing production growth	3.24	3.17	−6.40	9.45	21
Real growth rates in developing countries	4.89	1.60	1.70	8.40	35
Real export growth in developing countries	7.92	14.91	−21.56	35.43	35
Real growth rates in manufacturing export-based developing countries	5.62	1.38	2.69	8.62	35
Real manufacturing export growth in manufacturing export-based developing countries	8.12	13.99	−17.03	32.99	35
Real growth rates in commodity export-based developing countries	3.43	2.30	−1.93	8.18	35
Real commodity export growth in commodity export-based developing countries	7.36	19.64	−40.82	41.12	35

economic growth for both expansion and contraction phases (see the obtained minimum and maximum values) while the difference in their mean values is relatively small.

Before estimating the relationship between the two variables in the form of a model, it is important to test for their stationarity to avoid the problem of spurious regression. Since the data are already in the form of first differences, i.e., growth rates, the two variables are assumed to be stationary. This can be confirmed from a visual inspection of the data, i.e., an inspection of the correlogram, and an augmented Dickey-Fuller (ADF) test. The purpose of the ADF test is to see whether these variables exhibit unit root processes, as with the case of the random walk without drift (no constant and no time trend). The results of the ADF test are also given in Table A.5.2. They suggest that the null hypothesis can be rejected at the 99% level for both variables. That is to say, these two series are stationary, given that the obtained test statistics are smaller than their critical values.

The method chosen for testing the relationship between the two variables is OLS, and the specification of the model to be tested is informed by the theory and empirical analyses in Chapters 2 and 5. The relationship to be tested is the functional dependence of global real GDP growth (Y_t) on global manufacturing growth (X_t) t is time, α is the constant term, and since the relationship being tested is a

Table A.5.2 Test statistics for selected variables

	Test statistics	*Critical value*			*No. of obs.*
		1%	*5%*	*10%*	
Real global growth rates	−4.159	−3.75	−3	−2.63	20
Real global manufacturing production growth	−4.778				
Real growth rates in developing countries	−3.512	−3.689	−2.975	−2.619	34
Real export growth in developing countries	−3.797				
Real growth rates in manufacturing export-based developing countries	−4.216				
Real manufacturing export growth in manufacturing export-based developing countries	−3.731				
Real growth rates in commodity export-based developing countries	−4.325				
Real commodity export growth in commodity export-based developing countries	−3.892				

non-determinate one, an error term, μ is added (these three terms are used for all the equations below).

$$Y_t = \alpha + \beta X_t + \mu \quad \text{for } t = 1,\ldots,t \tag{A.1}$$

The estimation results of this error in the bracket is as follows:

$$\underset{(0.141)}{Y_t = 1.72} + \underset{(0.032)}{0.39X_t}, \ R^2 = 0.89, \ N = 21 \tag{A.2}$$

These results show the parameter estimate to be 0.39 and significant at the 99% level. This means that a 1% rise in global manufacturing growth can be argued to give rise to a 0.39% increase in global real GDP growth. To put this parameter value into some sort of context, it suggests the contribution of manufacturing to real GDP growth is higher than its weight in GDP would suggest. Indeed, it may be seen to be considerably higher than the relative and absolute contribution of the services sector, which accounts for some 70% of value added during this period.[17] The

R-squared for the co-movement of the two variables is 0.89, suggesting a high degree of explanatory power of the estimated equation.

Real GDP and export growth rates of groupings of developing countries

This section discusses the econometric evidence pertaining to the relationship between real GDP and export growth which is argued to exist to one degree or another for various groupings of developing countries. The clustering of countries to be considered in this section is that pertaining to different structures of developing country economies: (a) developing countries as a whole (combination of middle- and low-income countries), (b) manufacturing export-based, and (c) primary commodity export-based countries. This evidence can be seen as providing confirmation of the results obtained in Chapter 5 from exploratory data analysis. The data used for the econometric analyses are those used in the analyses of the corresponding relationships in Chapter 5. It should be recalled that the data used for that analysis are non-smoothed, weighted real GDP and export growth for each cluster.

Merchandise export growth of developing countries as a whole and their real GDP growth

Another important finding of Chapter 5 is that the growth impetus of the developing countries comes mainly from the advanced economies and is manifest in the relationship between the growth rates of these economies and their merchandise exports. To further investigate this relationship, the data used for the analysis are those depicted in Figure 5.5, the non-smoothed weighted real GDP growth rates and export growth rates of developing countries between 1983 and 2017 for which data are available. The descriptive statistics pertaining to these two series are presented in Table A.5.1. This table shows that the degree of movement in export growth in the developing countries is larger than the growth rates of the developing countries. In terms of the mean, the movement of the latter is double the former, while the minimum value of the latter is more than ten times greater, and its maximum value is around four times greater.

The estimation procedure begins with stationarity checks for the variables, i.e., the ADF test of these two series. The test statistics provided in Table A.5.2 suggest that the null hypothesis can be rejected and both series are stationary at 99% level.

The regression equation to be estimated by OLS[18] is the same as A.1 above and has as the dependent variable the real growth rates of developing countries (Y_t) and the independent variable the growth rates of their exports in constant dollars (X_t);

The estimation result obtained is

$$\underset{(0.228)}{Y_t = 4.31} + \underset{(0.014)}{0.074 X_t}, \; R^2 = 0.47, \; N = 35 \qquad \text{(A.3)}$$

The parameter estimate is 0.074, which is consistent with the relative proportions of the respective means of the two variables shown in Table A.5.2. This estimate is significant at the 99% level and confirms the positive relationship between economic growth and export growth of developing countries. The R-squared is a respectable 0.47. It needs noting that two modifications of the preceding model (one with the introduction of lagged variable to reflect the possible lead-lag relationship before 2000, and the other with the inclusion of dummy variable to account for the break in the contemporaneous relationship between 1992 and 1997) were also tested to see if they improved the goodness of fit. However, the neither of additional variable in either models is statistically significant and the adjusted R-squared hardly changed.[19]

Growth of manufacturing export-based developing countries and their export growth

For manufacturing export-based economies, the model to be estimated is the hypothesised relationship between weighted real GDP growth rates of these manufacturing export developing countries (Y_t) and their weighted real export growth rates (X_t), using equation depicted in A.1 above.

The descriptive statistics for these two variables are given in Table A.5.1. They show similar ratios between means and standard deviations for the two series as those shown for the series based on income levels. The results of the ADF test for the two variables are also shown in Table A.5.2. They confirm the stationarity for both variables at the 99% level.

The OLS estimation gives the following results:

$$\underset{(0.199)}{Y_t = 5.07} + \underset{(0.012)}{0.068 X_t}, \; R^2 = 0.47, \; N = 35 \qquad \text{(A.4)}$$

The estimated parameter value is shown to be statistically significant at the 99% level. The coefficient is slightly smaller than the estimated parameter value for the regression of total merchandise export growth on total real GDP growth for all developing countries (see equation A.3 above). This suggests that real GDP growth rates of commodity producers are likely to be more sensitive to their export growth rates than is the case for manufacturers—as is often argued in the literature on development.[20]

Since Figure 5.6 in Chapter 5 suggests that a lead-lag relationship between the two series seem to be more evident, which may have resulted in a lower parameter value for the contemporaneous relationship, a lagged dependent variable was introduced into the model. The regression equation to be estimated is

$$Y_t = \alpha + \beta_0 X_t + \beta_1 X_{t-1} + \mu \qquad \text{(A.5)}$$

The OLS estimation result is as follows:

$$\underset{(0.213)}{Y_t = 4.961} + \underset{(0.014)}{0.062X_t} + \underset{(0.014)}{0.018X_{t-1}},\ Adj\ R^2 = 0.47,\ N = 34 \qquad \text{(A.6)}$$

The results show that the parameter value of the lagged independent variable is not statistically significant, while that of the contemporaneous independent variable continues to be significant, but of a slightly lower value. The adjusted R-squared also slightly fell in comparison to the original model (see equation A.4), suggesting that the explanatory power of this modified model did not improve.

Growth of commodity export-based developing countries and their export growth

The second of the clusters of developing countries based on the structures of their production (exports) to be considered is those classified as commodity exporters. The model to be estimated is the hypothesised relationship between weighted real GDP growth rates of these commodity-exporting developing countries (Y_t) and their weighted real export growth rates (X_t); and the equation is the same as equation A.1.

The descriptive statistics and the results of the ADF test for these two variables are given in Table A.5.2. They show somewhat higher ratios of mean export growth rates of these developing countries to their real GDP growth rates as compared with those for manufacturing exporters. These results of the ADF test confirm the stationarity of the real growth rates and the real commodity export growth rates at the 99% level.

The results for the OLS regression of the real growth rates of commodity-producing countries on their export growth rates are as follows:

$$\underset{(0.34)}{Y_t = 2.925} + \underset{(0.016)}{0.069X_t}, \; R^2 = 0.35, \; N = 35 \qquad \text{(A.7)}$$

The obtained statistically significant coefficient of 0.069 is slightly higher than that of the manufacturing-based developing economies.[21] This result suggests, as already concluded above, that GDP growth rates of commodity-based exporters are more sensitive to their export growth than manufacturing-based exporters. This confirms general perceptions of non-mainstream development economists, that supply tends to be relatively price inelastic for commodity producers (see, for example, Kenyon, 1979). It should be noted that the introduction of a lagged independent variable and dummy variable did not improve the explanatory power of the model.

Notes

1 For the study on the drivers of cycles for selected individual developing countries, see Ikeda (2018). The analysis of the drivers of cycles in individual developing countries sought to expand on the findings of drivers of cycles pertaining to clusters of developing countries.

2 It is important to reiterate the point made in Chapter 1; that the aim of this chapter is not to explain the causes and transmissions of cycles in general.

3 Data pertaining to real manufacturing production in the Chinese economy are not directly provide by the World Bank; these data therefore had to be computed by the author drawing from the raw data provided by the World Bank (data accessed 21 March 2019).

4 While the correlation does not imply the causal relationship, the close synchronisation between the two variables are confirmed with the high correlation coefficient of 0.95 for the same period.

5 Countries included are Cambodia, Democratic People's Republic of Korea, Hong Kong SAR, India, Indonesia, Lao PDR, Macau SAR, Malaysia, Mongolia, Myanmar, Philippines, Republic of Korea, Thailand, Timor-Leste, and Vietnam.

6 Author's calculation based on World Bank data (data accessed 21 March 2019).

7 The result of the analyses with the weighted global cycles is similar.

8 Evidence for the expansionary policies implemented by the Chinese authorities has been provided by a number of business economists (see, for example, Wildau, 2016; Davis, 2017).

9 Data accessed 7 April 2019.

10 Recent data suggest that among the advanced countries Japan and the EU as a block (consisted of Germany, France, and Italy), and Germany in

particular, has come to be most closely aligned to the Chinese economy. For example, the correlation coefficients for the growth rates of the EU, Germany, Japan and the U.S. economies with that of the Chinese economy over the period between 2010 and 2017 are 0.47, 0.69, 0.46 and minus 0.02, respectively.

11 It can justifiably be argued that the Chinese economy is in turn dependent on demand from the advanced countries, particularly the U.S., for its export and real GDP growth. However, the point that is being made here is that notwithstanding where the demand for its products is coming from, as the largest manufacturer it appears to have the biggest influence on the growth of global GDP as a whole, and, most importantly, on the growth of the vast majority of (developing) countries making up the global economy. This is perhaps best evidenced by the post-2011 period when the growth rates of most developing countries fell with that of the Chinese economy, notwithstanding the relatively stable growth of the U.S. economy.

12 The analysis of the link between real GDP and export earnings growth rates of this aggregate cluster of developing countries will serve as a benchmark for the analysis of similar links pertaining to various sub-divided clusters of developing countries.

13 See Ikeda (2018) for the analyses for the breakdown with middle- and low income-countries. It was shown that the relationship between the growth rates and export growth was relatively stronger for middle-income countries as compared with low-income countries. It is of note that most exporters of manufactures tended to be middle-income countries, although the latter are not the same as the former.

14 See Ikeda (2018) for the analyses of individual sub-divided clusters such as food, fuel, and ores and metals. The analyses suggest some variation in degrees of synchronisation between economic and export growth rates. In particular, the weakest synchronisation to be for food exporters and the strongest for fuel exporters. This is to be expected given, on the one hand, the vagaries of natural conditions for the former, and, on the other, the degree of specialisation typically associated with the latter group of countries.

15 The relatively higher magnitude of the parameter value is due to the greater volatility of export growth without having any implication for the relative significance of the relationship.

16 Although the greater volatility in the prices of commodities can be attributed to some extent to the speculative activity of commodity traders, there can be little doubt that for the most part, and over the longer term, it has to do with their relative inelasticity of supply.

17 Based on the author's calculation with the value added of different sectors at current U.S. dollar prices.

18 For this estimation, while the data period is up to 2013, panel data regression methods were also used. The OLS method was used to support the finding of the apparent long-run relationship between the two variables (depicted in Figure 5.5), and panel data regression methods were used to allow for heterogeneity in the years and countries included in the regression analysis. See further details, Ikeda (2018).

19 See more details of these estimation, Ikeda (2018).

20 The comparison of the parameter values is formally premised on a prior simple *t*-test of the statistical significance of the mean difference between the parameter estimates. This test confirms, as one would expect given that manufacturing countries are a sub-set of all developing countries, that the mean difference is statistically different from zero. Although it is recognised that there are more robust tests available (e.g., use of a condition variable), it is felt that these are unwarranted given the above-mentioned fact that manufacturing countries are a sub-set of all developing countries and the *a priori* economic reasoning used in the formulation of these and other regressions undertaken in this section.

21 See note 20 for the testing method. The statistical significance is confirmed in this test as well.

References

Davis, G. (2017) 'China credit squeeze dents global growth', *Financial Times*, 7 May 2017, Available at www.ft.com/content/947e751f-c9d7-37f6-bf7b-8843da41e258 [Retrieved 10 May 2015].

Hausmann, R., Hwang, J. and Rodrik, D. (2007) 'What you export matters', *Journal of Economic Growth*, 12(1), 1–25.

Ikeda, E. (2018, September) *Global and Developing Country Business Cycles* (Den Haag: International Institute of Social Studies, Erasmus University Rotterdam), Doctoral dissertation, Available at https://repub.eur.nl/pub/110795 [Retrieved 15 June 2019].

Kenyon, P. (1979) 'Pricing', in Eichner, A.S. (ed.) *A Guide to Post-Keynesian Economics* (New York: M. E. Sharpe), pp. 35–36.

Rodrik, D. (2007) 'Industrial development: Some stylized facts and policy directions' in United Nations *Industrial Development for the 21st Century: Sustainable Development Perspectives* (New York: United Nations), pp. 7–28.

Wildau, G. (2016) 'China deploys state enterprises to economic stimulus effort', *Financial Times*, 21 June 2016, Available at www.ft.com/content/3d10e5cc-3754-11e6-a780-b48ed7b6126f [Retrieved 10 April 2017]

Databases

Board of Governors of the Federal Reserve System (FED). 'Foreign exchange rates' www.federalreserve.gov/releases/h10/summary/indexb_m.htm

OECD.Stat. Composite Leading Indicators (MEI) http://stats.oecd.org/Index.aspx?DataSetCode=MEI_CLI

World Development Indicators (WDI). http://databank.worldbank.org/data/reports.aspx?source=world-development-indicators

6 Summary, conclusions, theoretical and policy implications, and avenues for future research

Introduction

The aim of this final chapter is fourfold: first, to summarise the key findings with respect to the major objectives posed at the outset; second, to indicate its contribution to the already considerable and rapidly expanding corpus of literature on the subject; third, to draw out clearly certain theoretical and policy implications of the present study for the understanding of cycles, especially those at the global level and in (the sub-global groupings of) developing countries; and lastly, to provide a number of suggestions for possible future directions of research on the subject.

Main findings

The objectives posed at the outset of the book indicated the focus of the study to be: the conceptualisation of cycles and how this informs the present study of cycles in developing countries; and the identification, nature and drivers of cycles at the global level and developing country clusters. The major findings will be summarised with respect to each of these in turn.

Conception of cycles

In the discussion of the basic generic conception of cycles, it was argued that these need to be understood as **recurrent but non-regular (i.e., non-periodic) and non-symmetric** alternating sequences of expansionary and contractionary economic activity. These sequences need to be seen as conditioned by long-term trends in economic activity (and, in turn, as conditioning the long-term trends in this activity), as well as being the product of the workings of the economic system and integral to it. It was argued that this conception is fundamentally different to that of orthodox mainstream studies, which typically see cycles as non-recurrent random fluctuations in economic activity resulting from various and varied 'shocks' to the system which are exogenous to its workings and have no bearing on any long-term trends in this activity. It was further argued that the alternative conception accepts the fact that such shocks that cause the fluctuation that is having a bearing on the cyclical movements exist, but posits that they cannot be seen as the triggers of *repeated cycles*. Indeed, it was noted that, for many orthodox economists, this conceptualisation of cycles as fluctuations results in a denial of the existence of cycles. Some mainstream approaches, most notably the so-called modern classical cycle approach, dissents from this view, arguing, in keeping with the overwhelming evidence, and even methods used to identify cycles, that such fluctuations are recurrent and have a certain periodicity. However, they stop short of arguing, in the manner of Classical economists, that such cycles in economic activity are inherent to the system, leaving open the possibility of seeing them as the product of repeated shocks. It was further noted that, somewhat paradoxically, the implicit conception of cycles underlying many mainstream cycle identification methods is that of recurrent and even symmetric fluctuations in economic activity that are, by implication, endogenous to the system rather than random fluctuations which are exogenous to it.

The alternative generic conception of cycles was then used as a basis for conceptualising global cycles and cycles pertaining to groupings of countries. It was argued that: a) global cycles should be seen as the synchronised, alternating, recurrent, but non-periodic and non-symmetric movements in economic activity of all or most countries comprising the global economy; b) cycles pertaining to groupings of countries should be seen as synchronised, alternating, recurrent, but non-periodic and non-symmetric movements in the economic activity of all or most countries comprising clusters of economies.

Identification and existence of cycles

The alternative conception of the cycle, together with the critique of mainstream cycle methods of cycle identification, was used as a basis for the development of an alternative method for cycle identification. The main criticism of mainstream cycle identification methods, especially HP and BP filters, was their implicit presumption and imposition of regularity and symmetry in the cycles to be identified, contrary to the evidence of cycles being non-regular and non-symmetric.

The alternative conceptualisation of the cycle and the criticism of mainstream methods of cycle identification suggested the need for the development of alternative, less deterministic, and less mechanical methods for cycle identification. The alternative proposed was the use of real GDP growth rates, non-linear trends, and cycle troughs in these growth rates for the identification of generic cycles. It was argued that, notwithstanding its many known problems, the appropriate variable for identifying the cycle is the real GDP growth rate, simply because it remains the best available single variable which captures general economic activity, and also comparable. In order to avoid eliminating and distorting crucial information contained in the actual data, data transformations and smoothing techniques, as argued, will not be used. Emphasis was placed on the use of non-linear trends to emphasise the importance of path dependency in the identification of cycles as alternating periods of expansion and contraction in economic activity with respect to a longer-term (path-dependent) trend. To serve to highlight the importance of path dependency, in contrast to the standard practice in the existing studies of separating cyclical from trend movements or use linear estimation techniques to identify trends, the appropriate trend was conceived of as a moving average. Attention was also drawn to the importance of not identifying cycle peaks and troughs with the use of mathematical *maxima* and *minima*, respectively, since periods of economic strength and weakness were seen as likely to continue for varied periods of time after cycle *maxima* and *minima* were reached, leading to a confusion of cycles with fluctuations.

The alternative methods for the identification of generic cycles were then extended to provide a methodology for the identification of cycles at the global level and pertaining to sub-global groupings of countries. For the identification of these cycles, it was argued that it is necessary to show, first, that there are cycles in aggregate economic activity at these two levels (taking the weighted average growth rates of the countries comprising the clusters, in the case of cycles pertaining to sub-global groupings of countries) in accordance with the alternative criteria developed for the identification of cycles in general, and, second, that these cycles correspond to the synchronised cyclical movements in the (majority of) individual countries comprising the clusters (taking the non-weighted average growth rates of the countries comprising the clusters) and serving as the benchmark or reference.

Using these alternative methods of cycle identification, global cycles were shown to exist. Specifically, the cyclical growth rates of aggregate non-weighted real GDP of all countries comprising the global economy were shown to move together with cyclical growth rates in aggregate weighted real GDP of these countries, although some divergence in the two series was noted in recent years. This was argued to be a remarkable finding, since it suggests that there is a global economic force acting on all economies, irrespective of their size. Cycles were then identified for different sub-global groupings of countries based on levels of development (i.e., advanced and developing countries) and economic structure (i.e., manufacturing- and primary goods-based export developing countries). It was argued that these characteristics need to be taken into account when identifying cycles, since they can be expected to have a considerable bearing on the cyclical movement of these economies. It was found, as one might also have expected, that advanced and manufacturing economies are more synchronised with the global cycles than developing countries and primary commodity producers. It was, in fact, noted that cycle identification in the latter group was often difficult due to the greater susceptibility of their growth rates to the impacts of all manner of random (domestic) shocks.

Drivers of cycles

Although potentially vast, the discussion of the drivers of cycles was limited to the country drivers of the global cycles, and the extent of the influence of the latter on cycles in developing countries.

It was found that, contrary to common perceptions, the major country drivers of global cycles have not been the largest advanced economies *per se* but rather the largest manufacturing economies. Although for most of the time period under consideration, the two could be taken as synonymous, at certain junctures there is an important distinction to be made between the two. The particular significance of the distinction was argued to be best understood in the context of the recent rise of China as the global manufacturing powerhouse, notwithstanding its developing country status, and the implications this appears to be having on our understanding of the dynamics of the global economy. Specifically, it was argued that there is a growing body of evidence suggesting that the movements of global cycles are increasingly more in tune with the movement of the Chinese economy, which has become the largest manufacturing producer, than with the large advanced country economies, e.g., the United States or Europe. This link was argued to be most clearly evident in the period from cycle V (2009 onwards), with the weakening of the Chinese economy especially in the period after 2011 seen to have a depressive effect on most developing country economies, in spite of the steady growth of the U.S. economy—traditionally seen as providing the major impetus to movements in the global economy.

The major driver of cycles pertaining to sub-global groupings of developing countries was shown to be the global economy and, in particular, impulses emanating from the external environment *via* trade channels. It was shown that, for all developing countries, there is a close relation between the weighted growth rates of real GDP and exports and, where the movement of the two is not synchronised, it is export growth that leads economic growth. This relationship was then shown to hold, to differing degrees, when developing countries are broken down into different clusters based on different levels of development (per capita income) and structures of production (or structures of merchandise exports to be precise).

Key contributions

The study can be argued to make a number of important contributions to the literature on business cycles in general, and that on global and developing country cycles in particular. These contributions can be listed as follows.

The first contribution is the alternative conception of cycles, and the distinction to be drawn between cycles and fluctuations. It was argued that the alternative conception of cycles and the implied distinction between cycles and fluctuations have far-reaching and profound consequences for their identification and the explanations of their drivers.

The second contribution to the literature on business cycles is the proposed alternative method for their generic identification, founded on the alternative conception noted above. This method eschews the use of filters and the like in favour of a less technically robust but more qualitatively informed method. It was shown that this alternative method of identification, and in particular the use of non-linear trends in identification, implicitly recognises cycles as path dependent and not movements around an independent trend.

The third contribution to the literature on business cycles is the method proposed for the identification of global (and sub-global) cycles: that is, the use of non-weighted aggregate growth rates of countries comprising the global economy. Most studies take weighted average growth rates, with weights being assigned on the basis of country size.

The fourth, and related, contribution is the actual identification of global (and sub-global) cycles using non-weighted growth rates. An important implication of this finding is that it indicates the existence of a global gravitational economic force operating on all economies, regardless of the sizes of economies, including the advanced economies.

The fifth contribution of the study to the literature is the importance ascribed to manufacturing economies as the drivers of the global cycles. This contribution is founded on the somewhat unfashionable and nowadays unconventional view that it is the growth of the manufacturing sector which typically drives economic growth.

The sixth and last contribution to be noted is the importance to be ascribed to global cycles in understanding the movement of cycles in developing countries, with differences between the movement of developing country cycles in relation to the global cycles being dependent on levels of development and the structures of economy.

Theoretical and policy implications

The study also has a number of important theoretical and policy implications which warrant some elaboration here. These follow from the findings regarding the conception, identification, and drivers of cycles at the global level and developing country clusters summarised above.

Theoretical implications

The first theoretical implication of the preceding study is that it serves to reinforce the standard non-mainstream view of the capitalist economic system as inherently unstable. Specifically, it suggests—as non-mainstream economists have long argued—that the recurrent cycles in economic growth rates (and other macroeconomic phenomena) result from the normal functioning of the system, although there are disagreements within the non-mainstream camp over whether the periodic crises accompanying these cycles in economic growth rates are necessary for the functioning of the system. This brings into question the basic validity of many mainstream macroeconomic analyses and models, even those which accept the existence of cycle phenomena, since they are all premised in one way or another on the assumption of stable economic growth as the normal state of affairs. It suggests that these analyses and models paint an essentially misleading picture of the capitalist economy.

A second theoretical implication of the study is the need for a distinction to be drawn between cycles and random fluctuations.

The third theoretical implication to be drawn from the study is the importance to be attached to the global macroeconomic environment when analysing and projecting macroeconomic trends in the global economy. It was shown that cyclical trends in growth rates of most countries comprising the global economy tend to move together, suggesting that the global economy is exerting some sort of gravitational force on all its constituent countries. Many mainstream and non-mainstream analyses and models of the macroeconomic dynamics of economies pay little or no heed to this global gravitational force, and those that do tend to accord it only a marginal significance. That is to say, these analyses and models are failing to spot the elephant in the room.

The fourth theoretical implication that needs to be drawn from the study is the importance of manufacturing production in general, and large manufacturing-based economies in particular (and most notably China in the recent past), in driving the cycles in global economic growth. Evidence suggests that manufacturing economies are more cyclical than commodity-exporting economies because they are more income elastic than the latter. Although there are a large number of studies that attest to the importance of manufacturing production in driving economic growth in individual countries and even clusters of countries, there are few if any that extend this to the global economic setting and the global economic growth cycle. Indeed, most attention is typically paid to cyclical movements in global aggregate demand and to aggregate demand in the large advanced economies, without any reference to the cyclical movements in global output of any particular sector. What the preceding study suggests is that, even if the focus is on the movement of global aggregate demand, it needs to be linked to corresponding movements in global manufacturing production and manufacturing-based economies in order to better understand the dynamics of global economic cycles (and the co-movement of growth rates of large numbers of economies). It is only this focus on manufacturing production that enables one to fully appreciate the fall in growth rates of the majority of developing countries in the period 2011–15, a period when the largest producer of manufactured commodities, China, experienced a protracted fall in its growth rate. China, as the largest producer of manufactures, is also the biggest buyer of raw materials, which are the mainstay of most developing countries. This explains the correlation between the fall in economic growth of the Chinese economy and that of these other economies.

The fifth theoretical implication to be derived from the preceding study is that developing countries also experience cycles (as opposed to random fluctuations) in their economic growth and that these cycles need to be understood with reference to the global economic cycle. This is in stark contrast to most mainstream views and analyses of growth processes in developing countries, which tend to see any cyclical phenomena as fluctuations in aggregate output which are largely the result of random domestic shocks—even when the importance of trade and capital flows for the domestic economy are formally acknowledged. This is evidenced by typical central bank and finance ministry reports in most developing countries where there is scarcely a reference to the global economic environment, except perhaps in a global crisis situation.

Policy implications in developing countries

The policy implications arising out of the study follow to a large extent, as one would expect, from the theoretical implications. To begin with, the study suggests that policy makers need to be more circumspect in their use of so-called Dynamic Stochastic General Equilibrium (DSGE) models, the models typically favoured by policy makers the world over, when making policy decisions. Although there is considerable variation among the models used in different countries, all these models typically assume the economic system to be largely stable, and certainly not characterised by non-periodic recurrent cycles. Thus, their attempts to extrapolate the timing of cyclical movements typically fail to capture the state of economies adequately. Although there is circumstantial evidence that some policy makers acknowledge the existence of recurrent cycles—for example, those belonging to the U.S. Federal Reserve—it is unclear to what extent this compensates for the prognoses and forecasts generated by the DSGE models they also rely on.

Second, the study suggests that policy makers, especially those in developing countries, should pay considerably more attention than they do at present to developments in the global economy when formulating macroeconomic policy. For example, when setting domestic growth targets and associated policies, policy makers would do well to pay heed to the current and projected global economic growth environment in order to avoid the possible adverse budgetary consequences of a major error in forecasts. The same can be said for inflation. There is now considerable evidence to show that inflation trends for most countries in the world are broadly similar, suggesting that in this case, too, external forces are at work and need to be taken into account when setting inflation targets and devising corresponding inflation policies.

Third, the observed increasing synchronisation of cycles suggests a need for greater macroeconomic policy coordination at the international level with a view to increasing stability in the global economy, especially among those countries which can be deemed to lie at the epicentre of the global economy—large manufacturing-based economies and those accepted as issuers of world money. This increasing coordination is already in evidence with respect to monetary policies but is also key with respect to fiscal policies.

Fourth, the study suggests that an important distinction needs to be made by policy makers between cycles and fluctuations, with the significance of this distinction for policy varying between advanced and developing countries. The study has shown the existence of synchronised movement with different characteristics among the different clusters of economies, in particular those advanced (manufacturing based) countries emanate cyclical impulse and those developing countries are recipients of it. Thus, with respect to cycles, there is justification for the adoption of *ex ante* coordinated **countercyclical policies** in the advanced countries to prevent the cyclical downturn and *ex post* **mitigating policies** in the developing countries to ease the impact of cyclical movement, with the exception of China. With respect to fluctuations resulting from random shocks, there can only be *ex post* mitigating policies, whether in the advanced or developing countries. The *ex post* mitigating policies adopted in developing countries might include circumspect fiscal policies and a moderately accommodative monetary policy stance along with the strengthening of social safety nets to cushion somewhat the damaging consequences of a global slowdown or random domestic shock. Obviously, the space for individual countries to adopt such mitigating policies will depend on the particular situation of the country in terms of government debt, foreign exchange reserves, etc.

Future research possibilities

The preceding research has a great many implications for future research. The following are perhaps the most important of these. First, it suggests the need for an explanation of the trend element in cycle identification, possibly through the integration of the Juglar cycle analysis, which has been the focus of the present study, with what has been referred to as 'long-wave (-cycle)' analysis in the manner suggested by Joseph A. Schumpeter in his classic study of business cycles (1939; see also Chapter 1). Such an extension of the analysis would be particularly important for the identification of cycles in the advanced economies and at the global level, and consistent with the notion of path dependency in the derivation of growth rate trends.

Another direction in which the study could be extended is through the identification of cycle phases, particularly those preceding major turning points. A particularly promising line of research which accords with the identification methods favoured in the present study would be on what have been referred to as leading, lagging, and coincident indicators. Composites of such indicators are available for certain advanced countries, most notably the United States and Europe,[1] but few, if any, exist for global cycles as a composite. One of the problems with extending the existing indicators used in identification of cycles of advanced economies to the global level is that the theoretical basis for the construction of the composites is lacking. Clearly, this is something that will have to be delved into as part of any attempt to develop indicators for the identification of global cycle phases.

The study also suggests that more work needs to be done on the drivers of cycles, and in particular the transmission of cyclical impulses from the dominant economies to the developing economies. One question which needs more attention in this regard is why the movement of the Chinese economy appears to have such a disproportionate impact on the cyclical movement of most developing countries. Another is the nature of the transmission mechanisms from the advanced to the developing countries, and whether other financial flows, apart from those linked to trade in goods and services, have a bearing on the linkages between the advanced and developing countries.

Lastly, the study suggests that more work is needed on policy, and in particular the possible mitigating measures that could be taken by developing countries in a global cycle downturn. Traditionally, and as noted above, business cycle analysts have pointed to the relevance of cycle analyses for countercyclical measures. However, as was argued above, for developing countries the policy focus should be one of 'battening down the hatches'. For fiscal policy, this would mean considering the staggering or delaying of capital expenditures, delaying expansions in employment of government personnel, etc. In terms of monetary policy, it might mean providing more liquidity (or lengthening the time period of repurchase agreements) and concessional loan facilities for strategic (export-oriented) sectors. Equally important are the policies which strengthen social safety nets safeguarding those sections of the population on low incomes that are most vulnerable to a possible downturn in the global economy.

Note

1 See the existing indicators provided by Conference Board, ECRI, and European Commission as examples (see website links in Websites under References).

References

Schumpeter, J.A. (1939) *Business Cycles: A Theoretical, Historical and Statistical Analysis of the Capitalist Process*, first edition, Vol I (New York: McGraw-Hill).

Websites

Conference Board. Global business cycle indicators. www.conference-board.org/data/bci.cfm

ECRI. www.businesscycle.com/

European Commission. European Business Cycle Indicators. http://ec.europa.eu/economy_finance/publications/cycle_indicators/

Appendix

Table A.1 Country clusters based on income levels and structure of the economy (changes from the previous cycles)

Income level	*1983 (1987[a])–1993*	*1994–2001*	*2002–2009*	*2010–2017*
Advanced countries				
High	**40**	**43**	**55**	**70**
	American Samoa, Aruba, Australia, Austria, The Bahamas, Bahrain, Belgium, Bermuda, Brunei Darussalam, Canada, Channel Islands, Denmark, Faeroe Islands, Finland, France, Germany, Greenland, Guam, Hong Kong SAR (China), Iceland, Ireland, Isle of Man, Israel, Italy, Japan, Kuwait, Luxembourg, Netherlands, New Zealand, Norway, Qatar, Saudi Arabia, Singapore, Spain, Sweden, Switzerland, United Arab Emirates, United Kingdom, United States, Virgin Islands (United States)	**Added (8):** Andorra, Cayman Islands, Cyprus, French Polynesia, Liechtenstein, Macao SAR (China), Monaco, Portugal **Deleted (5):** American Samoa, Bahrain, Guam, Isle of Man, Saudi Arabia	**Added (11):** Antigua and Barbuda, Bahrain, Barbados, Greece, Guam, Isle of Man, Rep. Korea, Malta, New Caledonia, Puerto Rico, San Marino, Slovenia **Deleted (0)**	**Added (16):** Croatia, Curacao, Czech Republic, Equatorial Guinea, Estonia, Gibraltar, Hungary, Northern Mariana Islands, Oman, Poland, Saudi Arabia, Sint Maarten (Dutch part), Slovak Republic, St. Martin (French part), Trinidad and Tobago, Turks and Caicos Islands **Deleted (1):** Antigua and Barbuda

(*Continued*)

Income level	1983 (1987[a])–1993	1994–2001	2002–2009	2010–2017
Developing countries				
Middle	**Total**			
(upper- and lower-)	**72**	**95**	**86**	**109**
	Manufacturing-based economies			
	14	**29**	**43**	**43**
	Barbados, Cyprus, Greece, Hungary, Rep. Korea, Macao SAR, Malta, New Caledonia, Portugal, Jamaica, Jordan, Morocco, South Africa, Turkey	**Added (19):** Brazil, Croatia, Czech Republic, Dominican Republic, Indonesia, Latvia, Lithuania, Malaysia, Mauritius, Mexico, North Macedonia, Philippines, Poland, Romania, Slovak Republic, Suriname, Tunisia, Uruguay **Deleted (4):** Cyprus, Macao SAR, New Caledonia, Portugal,	**Added (20):** Albania, Armenia, Belarus, Botswana, Bulgaria, Cabo Verde, China, Colombia, Costa Rica, Dominican Republic, Arab Rep. Egypt, El Salvador, Estonia, Eswatini, Lebanon, Namibia, Samoa, Sri Lanka, St. Kitts and Nevis, West Bank and Gaza **Deleted (6):** Barbados, Greece, Indonesia, Rep. Korea, Malta, Suriname	**Added (10):** Bhutan, Bosnia and Herzegovina, Georgia, Guatemala, India, Indonesia, Lesotho, Pakistan, Senegal, Vietnam **Deleted (10):** Armenia, Cabo Verde, Colombia, Croatia, Czech Republic, Estonia, Eswatini, Hungary, Poland, Slovak Republic

Primary commodity-based economies			
42	**30**	**32**	**47**
Algeria, Argentina, Belize, Bolivia, Brazil, Chile, Colombia, Rep. Congo, Costa Rica, Cote d'Ivoire, Dominica, Dominican Republic, Ecuador, Arab Rep. Egypt, El Salvador, Fiji, Gabon, Guatemala, Honduras, Kiribati, Libya, Malaysia, Mexico, Nicaragua, Oman, Panama, Papua New Guinea, Paraguay, Peru, Philippines, Samoa, Seychelles, St. Kitts and Nevis, St. Lucia, Syrian Arab Republic, Thailand, Tonga, Trinidad and Tobago, Tunisia, Uruguay, Vanuatu, Venezuela	**Added (5):** Bahrain, Grenada, Moldova, Saudi Arabia, St. Vincent and the Grenadines **Deleted (17):** Brazil, Rep. Congo, Cote d'Ivoire, Dominican Republic, Arab Rep. Egypt, Honduras, Libya, Malaysia, Mexico, Nicaragua, Papua New Guinea, Philippines, Samoa, Syrian Arab Republic, Thailand, Tunisia, Uruguay	**Added (10):** Cuba, Guyana, Honduras, Islamic Rep. Iran, Iraq, Kazakhstan, Maldives, Russian Federation, Suriname, Uruguay **Deleted (8):** Bahrain, Colombia, Costa Rica, El Salvador, Kiribati, Moldova, St. Kitts and Nevis, Vanuatu	**Added (22):** Angola, Antigua and Barbuda, Armenia, Azerbaijan, Cabo Verde, Cameroon, Columbia, Rep. Congo, Cote d'Ivoire, Ghana, Kiribati, Lao PDR, Libya, Mauritania, Moldova, Nicaragua, Nigeria, Sao tome and Principe, Sudan, Vanuatu, Rep. Yemen, Zambia **Deleted (7):** Cuba, Gabon, Grenada, Guatemala, Oman, Saudi Arabia, Trinidad and Tobago

(Continued)

Income level	*1983 (1987[a])–1993*	*1994–2001*	*2002–2009*	*2010–2017*
	N/A			
	16	**36**	**11**	**19**
	Antigua and Barbuda, Eswatini, Gibraltar, Grenada, Islamic Rep. Iran, Iraq, Lebanon, Mauritius, Poland, Puerto Rico, Romania, Senegal, St. Vincent and the Grenadines, Suriname, Rep. Yemen, Zimbabwe	**Added (30):** American Samoa, Angola, Belarus, Botswana, Bulgaria, Cabo Verde, Cuba, Djibouti, Estonia, Guam, Isle of Man, Kazakhstan, Dem. People's Rep. Korea, Libya, Maldives, Marshall Islands, Fed. Sts. Micronesia, Namibia, New Caledonia, Northern Mariana Islands, Papua New Guinea, Russian Federation, Samoa, Slovenia, Solomon Islands, Syrian Arab Republic, Turkmenistan, Ukraine, Uzbekistan, West Bank and Gaza **Deleted (10):** Gibraltar, Grenada, Mauritius, Poland, Romania, Senegal, St. Vincent and the Grenadines, Suriname, Rep. Yemen, Zimbabwe	**Added (4):** Bosnia and Herzegovina, Kiribati, Palau, Vanuatu **Deleted (29):** Angola, Antigua and Barbuda, Belarus, Botswana, Bulgaria, Cabo Verde, Cuba, Estonia, Eswatini, Guam, Islamic Rep. Iran, Iraq, Isle of Man, Kazakhstan, Dem. People's Rep. Korea, Lebanon, Maldives, Namibia, New Caledonia, Papua New Guinea, Puerto Rico, Russian Federation, Samoa, Slovenia, Solomon Islands, Syrian Arab Republic, Ukraine, Uzbekistan, West Bank and Gaza	**Added (13):** Cuba, Eswatini, Gabon, Grenada, Kosovo, Mongolia, Montenegro, Papua New Guinea, Serbia, Solomon Islands, Timor-Leste, Tuvalu, Uzbekistan **Deleted (5):** Bosnia and Herzegovina, Kiribati, Libya, Northern Mariana Islands, Vanuatu

Low	**Total**			
	49	**64**	**64**	**35**
	Manufacturing-based economies			
	4	**10**	**13**	**7**
	Bangladesh, India, Nepal, Pakistan	**Added (7):** Bhutan, Central African Republic, China, Arab Rep. Egypt, Haiti, Senegal, Sri Lanka **Deleted (1):** Pakistan	**Added (9):** Cambodia, Georgia, Indonesia, Kyrgyz Republic, Lesotho, Pakistan, Togo, Vietnam, Zimbabwe **Deleted (6):** Bhutan, China, Arab Rep. Egypt, Haiti, Nepal, Sri Lanka	**Added (2):** Madagascar, Nepal **Deleted (8):** Central African Republic, Georgia, India, Indonesia, Lesotho, Pakistan, Senegal, Vietnam
	Primary commodity-based economies			
	13	**13**	**30**	**17**
	Burkina Faso, Equatorial Guinea, Ghana, Indonesia, Kenya, Liberia, Madagascar, Malawi, Nigeria, Sierra Leone, Solomon Islands, Sri Lanka, Togo	**Added (9):** Benin, Burundi, Rep. Congo, Honduras, Mozambique, Nicaragua, Sudan, Uganda, Zimbabwe **Deleted (9):** Burkina Faso, Equatorial Guinea, Ghana, Indonesia, Liberia, Nigeria, Sierra Leone, Solomon Islands, Sri Lanka	**Added (22):** Azerbaijan, Burkina Faso, Cameroon, Comoros, Cote d'Ivoire, Ethiopia, The Gambia, Guinea, Kenya, Mali, Mauritania, Moldova, Mongolia, Niger, Nigeria, Papua New Guinea, Rwanda, Sao Tome and Principe, Sierra Leone, Tanzania, Rep. Yemen, Zambia **Deleted (5):** Rep. Congo, Honduras, Kenya, Togo, Zimbabwe	**Added (3):** Afghanistan, Central African Republic, Myanmar **Deleted (16):** Azerbaijan, Cameroon, Cote d'Ivoire, Guinea, Madagascar, Mauritania, Moldova, Mongolia, Nicaragua, Nigeria, Papua New Guinea, Sao Tome and Principe, Sierra Leone, Sudan, Rep. Yemen, Zambia

(*Continued*)

Income level	*1983 (1987[a])–1993*	*1994–2001*	*2002–2009*	*2010–2017*
	N/A			
	32	**41**	**21**	**11**
	Afghanistan, Benin, Bhutan, Burundi, Cambodia, Central African Republic, Chad, China, Comoros, Dem. Rep. Congo, Ethiopia, The Gambia, Guinea-Bissau, Guyana, Haiti, Lao PDR, Lesotho, Maldives, Mali, Mauritania, Mozambique, Myanmar, Niger, Rwanda, Sao Tome and Principe, Somalia, Sudan, Tanzania, Uganda, Vietnam, Zambia	**Added (19):** Albania, Armenia, Azerbaijan, Bosnia and Herzegovina, Burkina Faso, Cameroon, Cote d'Ivoire, Equatorial Guinea, Eritrea, Georgia, Ghana, Kyrgyz Republic, Liberia, Mongolia, Nigeria, Pakistan, Sierra Leone, Tajikistan, Rep. Yemen **Deleted (10):** Benin, Bhutan, Burundi, Central African Republic, China, Haiti, Maldives, Mozambique, Sudan, Uganda	**Added (9):** Angola, Bhutan, Rep. Congo, Haiti, Dem. People's Rep. Korea, Nepal, Solomon Islands, Timor-Leste, Uzbekistan **Deleted (29):** Albania, Armenia, Azerbaijan, Bosnia and Herzegovina, Burkina Faso, Cambodia, Cameroon, Comoros, Cote d'Ivoire, Ethiopia, The Gambia, Georgia, Guinea, Guyana, Kyrgyz Republic, Lesotho, Mali, Mauritania, Mongolia, Niger, Nigeria, Pakistan, Rwanda, Sao Tome and Principe, Sierra Leone, Tanzania, Vietnam, Rep. Yemen, Zambia	**Added (2):** Guinea, Sierra Leone **Deleted (12):** Afghanistan, Angola, Bhutan, Rep. Congo, Equatorial Guinea, Ghana, Lao PDR, Myanmar, Nepal, Solomon Islands, Timor-Leste, Uzbekistan

N/A	**53** Albania, Andorra, Angola, Armenia, Azerbaijan, Belarus, Bosnia and Herzegovina, British Virgin Islands, Bulgaria, Cabo Verde, Cayman Islands, Croatia, Cuba, Curacao, Czech Republic, Djibouti, Eritrea, Estonia, Georgia, Kazakhstan, Dem. People's Rep. Korea, Kosovo, Kyrgyz Republic, Latvia, Liechtenstein, Lithuania, Marshall Islands, Fed. Sts. Micronesia, Moldova, Monaco, Mongolia, Montenegro, Namibia, Nauru, North Macedonia, Northern Mariana Islands, Palau, Russian Federation, San Marino, Serbia Sint Maarten (Dutch part), Slovak Republic, Slovenia, South Sudan, St. Martin (French part), Tajikistan, Timor-Leste, Turkmenistan, Turks and Caicos Islands, Tuvalu, Ukraine, Uzbekistan, West Bank, and Gaza	**15** **Added (1):** Gibraltar **Deleted (39):** Albania, Andorra, Angola, Armenia, Azerbaijan, Belarus, Bosnia and Herzegovina, Bulgaria, Cabo Verde, Cayman Islands, Croatia, Cuba, Czech Republic, Djibouti, Eritrea, Estonia, Georgia, Kazakhstan, Dem. People's Rep. Korea, Kyrgyz Republic, Latvia, Liechtenstein, Lithuania, Marshall Islands, Fed. Sts. Micronesia, Moldova, Monaco, Mongolia, Namibia, North Macedonia, Northern Mariana Islands, Russian Federation, Slovak Republic, Slovenia, Tajikistan, Turkmenistan, Ukraine, Uzbekistan, West Bank, and Gaza	**9** **Added (0)** **Deleted (6):** Palau, San Marino, Serbia, Timor-Leste, Turks and Caicos Islands, Tuvalu	**3** **Added (0)** **Deleted (6):** Curacao, Gibraltar, Kosovo, Montenegro, Sint Maarten (Dutch part), Sint Maarten (French part)

N/A indicates the numbers of countries where relevant data is not available.

a The data in 1987 is extended to 1983, which is the first year of cycle II.

Index

Note: Page numbers followed by "n" denote endnotes.

Printed in the United States
by Baker & Taylor Publisher Services